THE INTELLECTUAL SALESMAN:

THE DIFFERENCE THAT MAKES THE DIFFERENCE IN SALES

JEFF DELGADO

IME Publishing Group/ Jeff Delgado
Po Box 2583
Martinez, Ca. (4553
www.IMEPublishingGroup.com

Warning—Disclaimer
The purpose of this book is to educate and inspire. This book is not intended to give advice or make promises or guarantees that anyone following the ideas, tips, suggestions, techniques or strategies will have the same results as the people listed throughout the stories contained herein. The author, publisher and distributor(s) shall have neither liability nor responsibility to anyone with respect to any loss or damage caused, or alleged to be caused, directly or indirectly by the information contained in this book.

The Intellectual Salesman/ Jeff Delgado. —1st ed.
ISBN 978-0-692-33736-3

For information www.TheIntellectualSalesman.com

Edited by Rick Chavez
Book Layout and Cover design by Mike Driggers

First Edition: January 2015

DEDICATION

I would like to dedicate this book to my mother and father, Shirley & Rogelio Delgado. Although my parents were not in the sales business, they taught me the value of working hard and pursuing my dreams. Because of my parents, I am able to truly value my profession and cherish every moment in life.

In loving memory of:
My parents Shirley & Rogelio Delgado

ACKNOWLEDGEMENTS

My Wife: Emily Delgado
My Daughter: Shirley Delgado
The Togonon Family
The Delgado Family

Special Thanks
David, Anthony (Tuffy), Jonathan, Jennifer,
Julia (Juju) & my cousin Roger (Rog)

My life-long Business Partners & Best Friends
Robert Pallen, Carlos Quintero, Eric Antonio,
Mark Senores, Paul Calub, Rich Monasterial,
Mike Driggers & Randy Wilson

CONTENTS

FOREWORD

When the question "Why sales?" comes up, I can honestly say I never wanted to be in sales! My perception of a salesman was entirely negative. I looked at salespeople as fast talkers, all of them just out to make a buck!

I was influenced into sales by pure accident. I was working your typical cubicle job with an hour-long commute, two 15-minute breaks, an hour for lunch, laboring with co-workers and a boss. My typical daily routine consisted of waking up at 6:00am, driving to work by 9:00am, and arriving home at 6:30pm on a good day. This routine was my life. It was all I knew. It was comfortable. It was familiar. And I actually loved my job! I felt fortunate to even have a job, considering my limited college background and work experience. I was just grateful to have a job. For me, that was enough.

Until one day, when I met this distinct, sharp gentleman. He had an air of confidence that I had never seen in my life. Our office was hosting a meeting with an important group of individuals. It seemed as if the President of the United States was visiting. I asked a co-worker, "Who are these successful looking people?" But he had no clue. I was extremely curious to know who this group was that had our office in such a frenzy. They all looked so professional and put-together. I was completely astounded and wondered what their role was for our company.

I finally had the opportunity to introduce myself to one of the gentlemen while we were walking down the hall. "Excuse me, Sir. I want to introduce myself and ask what you do for our company." He replied, "Why do you ask?" I answered, "Because you look so cool and our office seems to treat you guys like royalty." He laughed and said, "I'm an Agent (Salesman)." I asked, "What is that?" He replied, "We are responsible for finding and serving clients. Actually, your office supports our clients and we appreciate all of you." I asked, "Do you like what you do?" He said, "No! I don't like what I do. I LOVE WHAT I DO!" I had never heard anyone in my office say they loved their job so I immediately researched the position and soon became a salesman myself.

I have now been in sales for more than 20 years! I have seen some amazing things because of it. I enjoyed the benefits of being a salesman—the fun, offers of accomplishment, unlimited opportunity, unmatched job security, increased income, freedom, flexibility and time.

I have also experienced the dark side of sales, including the challenges of recession, financial reversals, high demands and pressure, inconsistent cash flow, lack of balance, complaints, health issues and stress. After years of experience, acquiring hundreds of clients and training and mentoring thousands of agents, I have learned that you are responsible and held accountable for your own performance. It directly relates to your efforts.

Being a great salesman is only half of the journey, though. In this new economy, you must become an Intellectual

Salesman! It is the secret to success in sales. You can pick up any book on motivation, inspiration and passion if you want encouragement. I love these books! But the next level is tapping into the intellectual side of sales! Time and technology have changed this industry dramatically. Without adding the Intellectual Salesman Strategies, you may encounter more of the dark side of sales. This book was written to help you become an absolutely successful Intellectual Salesman! It's the difference that makes the difference in sales!

1

THE HIGHER LAW OF SALESMANSHIP

Have you ever worked a 9-to-5 job that you felt didn't pay you enough? I remember times when I'd work my butt off all week to get a measly $400-500 check at the end of the week. The work didn't match my pay. When I would go to the boss and ask for a better position that paid more, there was always a barrier. In sales, no one can limit how much money you earn.

I can honestly tell you there's no better profession than sales.

The truth is, getting into any business requires you to sell something. Even if you are working as an employee, you're selling your talent and your skills. The best profits for you or your company roll in when you're able to sell your products or services the right way.

After being in sales for so many years, I've learned that you need to be a combination of two types of people in order to succeed in this career field. One is the traditional salesman, the kind who sells things the old fashioned way. The good thing is they sell very well, are very good with people, very influential and confident, and they have the basic skills necessary and that's why they're successful. They're great at talking to people and are great influencers for customers who are making purchasing decisions.

Then there are those out there who may not be as strong at traditional sales but their skill set also helps them to be influential. They're very detail-oriented, what I would call intellectually focused. They may focus on calling ten people to get one bite. They work on ratios and scheduling in much more detail. You'll often see that type of sales person also doing well, even though they may lack some of the confidence and the influential qualities of the other group. But they still get great results, which is the bottom line.

The most successful salesmen are a combination of both personalities. They work their schedule, are very confident in what they do, and are very good with people. I call them Intellectual Professionals.

This type of salesman has the ability to do two things at once. It's not just a quick sales effort, merely trying to close the sale. This person is also very detailed and gets results that are long lasting.

Stability

Most traditional salesmen work at a variety of jobs, only settling down for a short while before their excitement level diminishes and they drift away again. These salesmen may have a great year, maybe a great month or a great quarter but then they're out. Many hate the job itself and are constantly trying to find another company to sell for.

Someone who's very intellectual, on the other hand, focuses on consistency so they seem to stay the course and have a longer career. Through personal experience, I've noticed that people who can mix those two styles well are the most successful. They're the ones who stay in the business, are consistent for a longer period of time, and enjoy a great career. That's why the mixture of the intellectual and the sales specialist is the ultimate professional salesman.

That type of salesman is like somebody who's great at art, who can create pottery and do all sorts of activities with their creative side, but they're also amazing with Calculus problems and scientific activities. They are left and right brain combined.

Of the two types of salesmen, the one with the organized intellectual side tends to adapt better in terms of focus. They tend to be very meticulous at their jobs, regardless of distractions. They just do the same thing over and over again.

The other type of salesmen dream a lot. They dream about what they want in their life, their goals, how much money they're going to make, and what their families are going to be able to buy. They dream more, but there may be a lack of focus and commitment.

New Age of Sales

Ten to 20 years ago, salesmen were selling much different things than they sell today. The world changes so quickly, there are jobs that didn't even exist ten years ago. That necessitates a change in sales mentality, sales strategy, and the approach of a salesman. You may be selling apps, you may be selling software, you may be selling highly technical projects compared to salesmen back in my Dad's era who were selling refrigerators and used cars and stuff like that. Does that necessitate a whole different type of sales mechanism?

I definitely think so. In the past decades, you could get away by just being really influential, just being a great guy and getting the client to like you. You could get away with a lot because clients didn't have the resources to research certain areas. The best way to research back in those days was the encyclopedia and even that was updated through a very slow process.

Today, if you're selling an app or a financial services program, the average consumer can research it on their own. So, you could be a great influencer but if you don't know your program and understand it thoroughly, your clients will buy it from a more informed competitor. Salesmen who know their products and who are likable will be the ones to make the sale. Customers can like you but still not do business with you if you don't know what you're talking about.

In today's world, with Google and Yahoo and other social media networks to help you get free information, you have to be sharper in terms of understanding your products, programs and strategies for clients. That gives an advantage to the intellectual side versus the sales side. That doesn't mean you need to know everything. It's just like selling cars. You don't need to know every detail about the engine or chassis, but there are areas of that car that you better know.

I was shopping for a television recently and walked into Best Buy but the salesman didn't know anything about the TV that I was looking at. I could tell the difference between him and another guy who did. I didn't buy from the salesman who didn't know his stuff.

There are certain times when I will buy an item just because I like the salesman. It's common with clothes; even if the salesman doesn't know where the shirt is made or who made it, I still buy the shirt because I like him. I may become the exception soon; because of the Internet, people are more discerning than ever and you must know your information in more detail.

People Skills

One of the things that stood out with the old-time salesmen was their ability to build a relationship. Back then relationship meant, "I sold you your last three cars" or "I sold you two or three washing machines". That trust was built over time. Internet time is so much faster but a strong relationship is still important.

There is an old saying that people don't care how much you know until they know how much you care. As you build relationships with your clients, they will return and give you repeat business and refer others. I totally believe that the referral side of the business is the major key to your success so make sure you're becoming a master at building relationships. Sometimes you can even get to a point where you become more than a salesman. You may become an information resource for your clients. If you are truly listening and caring about your clients, you'll succeed. I think that's how you get to be the best of the best.

Trust Building

Let's say you know the best place to get your car painted or the best place to buy tires. People you know will eventually need those services and you can become the go-to resource for that information. You're really good and you care and you build relationships, which allow you to get more from a client in the long run. I may sell you financial services programs but there are other areas that I don't cover, like trusts or wills or estate planning. I can refer clients to someone who actually does this and it builds a trust factor. Not only will they trust me but they'll also trust the people I refer to. I absolutely believe that relationships are still the key to building a winning sales practice.

Do You Care?

Most of my retirement planning clients are concerned about cash flow and where money's going to come from in the future. They're concerned about this because eventually they're going to have to stop working and their income will stop. So, the big question is how they're going to maintain their current lifestyle. The first questions I always get are, "Do you care?" and "Do you know what's going to happen tomorrow?" Will my program help themalleviate stress in the future?

When they come to seminars, they see retirementas something that they associate with a lot of pain. My job is to re-associate it with a positive feeling, a reassuring feeling that retirement can actually be a great thing. Retirement can be a dream come true.

There are certain areas I could focus on but I think the point of the seminar is to let them see where they can be, even though they may have doubts where they are or what they want to be. Let me give them good hope and directionand let them know that they can be in a great place. If they associate pleasure with meeting you, they'll want to meet with you again. In my seminars, my number one goal is to gain their trust so they'll say, "I just want to meet this guy, Jeff." If they like me and we meet again, they'll realize that truly do care.

I try to discover as much as I can about their situation so that's why I build a relationship first. I find out what their goals and dreams are and why they came to the seminar. Following that, I set up another session to develop a strategy based on the information they've given me. When I tell them that this strategy is based on what they've told me, most clients say, "Absolutely, that's what I am looking for." At that point we just achieved their stated goal and move closer to helping this clie.

These techniques work for everybody because we're all looking for either comfort or answers about the future. It's fundamental and bulletproof, regardless of whether you're selling cars, knives, life insurance or shoes. You have to go through the same cycle of caring for people and asking what they want. In the end, you're solving their problem. As salesmen, we are supposed to find what they're looking for.

Salesmen are problem solvers. When someone goes to buy a TV, their problem is either they don't like their current model or it's broken. There is a problem that we're trying to solve. A great salesman says, "I'll solve it better than anyone else you know." If you can prove that you care more than others, they'll buy from you.

I think the biggest challenge for salesmen today is just the number of competitors. If you have a lot of people who are selling a program like yours, and who may be more savvy in certain areas, you must get more people in front of you. Use the Internet and utilize social media to get in front of the competition, to see more people, and to build an advantage.

In my opinion, one of the things that people lack today is the passion for going all out. This world of sales is all about influence. If you are not organized and if you don't know your product and you are not detailed, consistent and focused, you may get shut out by someone who is.

You need to give everything and go all out. Know the strategy and the goals, then gain the confidence, consistency, discipline, and influence. If you have the passion and immerse yourself in it you will succeed at the highest level. You will be adhering to the Higher Law of Salesmanship.

2

TOP PRODUCER CHARACTERISTICS

The Number 1 characteristic of a top producer or leader is taking what they do seriously and planning everything. Success is no accident. I think many times the intellectual salesman is consumed with planning and execution, whereas, for lack of a better word, an amateur salesman would say, "I'm just going to go get it done. I'm just going to sell and close someone."

But when salesmen plan everything and take what they do very seriously, they're very meticulous in their movement and their daily activity. You will see much more intellect being applied rather than just trying to influence through persuasion.

I think, for most amateur salesmen, it's all about the money they need to make to reach their goals and needs for their families. As a professional, remember that your client must come first.

I would also suggest developing a positive business image. Do they see you as a person who is positive, whom they want to do business with? Do they perceive you as an expert in your industry? I think most don't become experts at what they sell.

They just say, "I'm going to close, it doesn't matter if I know everything about what I sell."

Today's top producers are experts in their programs and products, they're not just trying to sweet talk a guy into a sale. The intellectual salesmen will invest in themselves, not only in their businesses. I'm talking about investing in their own growth as a person, reading about their particular program, becoming stronger, knowing their competition and what's happening around them, and investing in time management and listening skills. They design a proper schedule that serves. An intellectual salesman will look at a jammed schedule and find out what needs fixing.

While most amateur salesmen just want to get the job done, an intellectual salesman asks, "Which areas could I improve on to increase my ratio? "If I have ten appointments and I close one, how do I up that to five instead?" Staying organized and thinking ahead is an intellectual skill that most people fail to focus on. Being organized and focused helps make sure each day is productive versus just breezing through it.

Goals

Your first priority as an intellectual salesman is to be clear about your goals. Most people don't know what they want so they just do whatever it takes to get to anywhere. They don't have a focused goal, there's no projection for what they're trying to do. They're not clear on anything.

Success could be simple small steps but some people are only looking at the big picture. In order for them to be successful, they think they need to be a millionaire. But what if they're only making $10 an hour today? If they were to start their own business and start making $20 an hour, they could be called successful because they're growing. The challenge is they don't have a crystal clear goal and they're not certain what they want. So, the first key is to find a goal and to have it written down so they know what they're going after and if they're growing towards that goal.

One of the problems is that we aren't being taught how to create goals when we're young. You may have been influenced by television, radio, and other media, which led you to follow their version of the American dream. We may have been taught to chase things but never to grow. I think one of the biggest challenges that we have to address as a society is learning how to grow on the inside first and then grow into our goals. I think many of you are facing these battles on the inside.

You'll see that with people who win the lottery or movie stars or athletes who receive a lot of money quickly. Without growing on the inside they eventually lose everything or, if they keep their money, they may lose in other areas of their life, whether it be their health, their family, their fitness, or just a sheer lack of balance. We've been taught to chase certain things in America but merely chasing things versus growing on the inside isn't the secret to success.

The challenge that most people have is the simple fundamental of writing down goals. The concept of creating goals has been written about in books for years but is still almost completely overlooked. No one really takes that seriously but it's ultimately the secret, at least from my own standpoint. It doesn't matter whether it's a three-to-five year plan or five-to-ten year plan, it needs to get done.

Written goals are not necessarily going to get you 100% there but you may get 90%. And if you do get 100%, wow, what a year, right? I don't see how anyone functions without goals. There was a line in a book that said, "A man without a goal is like a ship without a rudder. They both end up on the rocks." That's because there's no goal to pursue. I don't know how to function without that.

Someone once asked me, "Jeff, let's say I want to quit my job. I hate my job. I want to quit." Okay, then what's your financial goal? What do you need to make? Then I drilled down some more, "What is your weekly goal? What do you need to produce?" Then we went further, "What do you need to produce daily or even hourly?" Only then could I advise him what to do. It all comes down to the same thing. Without goals, you can only go so far in life and I think it's one of the ultimate secrets.

Confidence

There are certain characteristics that I believe you must have to move forward on this path. The first one is having confidence in what you do and who you are. You need to be crystal clear on who you are and what your stand in this business is. You need to have full confidence in what you sell and confidence in yourself that you can get it done.

When I started my selling career, I had no confidence and was so scared to meet a client. My first appointment was such a disaster that I almost wanted to quit. But over time and after many appointments I started to see positive results. Confidence comes from experience and grows as you endure in your sales career. Most people do not give their efforts enough time to compound. They will begin a sales career and do well in the first few tries, then suddenly have a bad month, lose all their confidence and quit the business.

You must understand that success has its ups and downs. In order to build confidence you must go through the tough times. In order to build strong confidence you must endure! Do you have the endurance and focus to gain the confidence necessary to take your business to the next level? To me, confidence means knowing deep down that you can find a way to make it through all adversity. Without confidence it will be impossible for you to succeed at the highest level.

Focus

Nobody but you can be responsible for your goals and what you produce for your family. If I have a situation where a manager is not leading me to success, I still must find the things that he does that are going to work for me and improve on the areas that he doesn't do very well. Let's say he's a good manager but when it comes to execution, he's weak. I won't focus on his execution, but I'll make sure that I take advantage of his stronger management skills.

If you're not focused, then you won't know what your priorities are and you won't be able to set realistic deadlines. I think setting my own deadlines is one of the biggest secrets of my entire career. If I had a priority checklist or, as I used to call it, 'Things I've Got To Get Done Today", it was the deadlines that were helping me. Let's say, for example, I was going to Hawaii in June. I knew what my deadline was to get in the best shape I could to look great in Hawaii. I set deadlines and would check them off weekly to note my progress. For people who try to achieve goals for their family or their business, it's the same thing. It's creating deadlines and setting priorities for those deadlines, and then reviewing your progress on a weekly or daily basis.

I have an assistant and she handles all my scheduling and makes sure my bills are paid. She makes sure every detail is taken care of, follows up on my appointments, sends thank you cards, and does other things that I just don't do. I leverage it to my full advantage.

Consistency

I've studied the things that highly successful salesmen have done throughout their careers and two of the major keys are consistency and finding a system that works for them. They're very well focused on a goal, whether it be daily, weekly, quarterly or annually. They may have small goals but they're very focused on them. Next is consistency to stay on track even when they face ups and downs. The challenge for those without a consistent plan is when they have a down period, will they give up, will they stop, or will they change their approach ? The successful ones are able to handle adversity as well as prosperity. Even if you're systematized you're still going to have adversity but many of the successful people I meet are successful because they're consistent and able to handle it. They don't kill their business; instead, they grow from it and then improve on it.

Consistency is priority-based. It's focusing on your goals and understanding what priorities you need to focus on and getting them done to reach the top. There are many new things that need to be done in order to get a sale, but there are certain ones that are consistent and never go away. One of them is your ability to get prospects in front of you. That is an area that must be consistently focused on. If you're always focusing on how to make a sale but you have no prospects, then you're ahead of yourself.

If your goal is to have X amount of sales, you better be consistent with prospecting, contacting and knowing how many presentations you've done before you start focusing on making a sale. Obviously, you're never going to get there without the prospects. So, consistency is knowing your priorities and executing them so that you get the results you want.

An intellectual salesman develops consistency over time. As an example, when you get up in the morning, you never miss brushing your teeth. No matter how rushed you are, you'll always take that minute or two to brush your teeth because the price you pay if you don't brush your teeth is high.

It's the same thing in sales, where you must learn good habits and be consistent at all times. Once you're consistent you have the ability to focus on your product. Most people fail to focus and keep their mind on one thing. Part of the problem I see is our growing fascination with the Internet and other general distractions.

When I was younger, there weren't any text messages to interrupt me in the middle of the day. But these days I receive emails all day long and they even show up on my phone screen. Everyone has cell phones so it's now possible to be interrupted any time of the day or night, if you allow it. Needless to say, I understand. The consistency to stay focused is very difficult in today's world.

Discipline

The next key is having the discipline to do the things you need to do on a daily basis. On that point alone I could go on forever, because I stress the need to discipline yourselves and do what you have to do, not what you want to do.

For example, let's say there are two guys who both want to be in great shape. One guy goes to the gym every single morning, the other guy doesn't. Most people think that the person who goes to the gym does it because he enjoys the workout. The truth is, most of the time he doesn't want to go but he disciplines himself to stay on the program. Just because that man hits the gym every day doesn't necessarily mean he wants to do it. But being disciplined means doing something that you have to do, not what you want to do.

Discipline is very critical when you're on a diet. If you eat right every single day, you'll find yourself in great shape. But if you're constantly cheating on your diet, you'll find yourself out of shape or sick. I think sales or running a business is very similar to health. Some people have disciplines that are not serving them while others who are successful have disciplines that are helping them make progress. You can't only be disciplined whenever it's convenient.

I think discipline is overlooked because it can truly be very simple. Success means following through on daily disciplines every single day, doing what you know you need to do, even though you don't want to do it.

It's easy in the sales world to prospect, get a list and make the calls. However, most won't do it because they associate prospecting with failure. They don't like to be rejected, so they don't make the calls. They don't want the result of a call to be hearing a prospect saying No. Those who don't make this simple phone call need to learn how to overcome that fear. But because they are not disciplined to do it consistently, they just push it aside.

Discipline is just doing simple things every single day. Like anything else, even having a great relationship requires simple discipline to take care of your spouse or to spend time with your children. It's always simple, never, "I've got to take them to Hawaii over the weekend," or "I've got to take my wife out to an exotic island," or "I've got to take her to this fancy restaurant." How about just taking her to a nice restaurant once in a while or paying attention to her when she comes home?

Are you willing to do the things that you don't want to do in order to get the results that you want? Are you willing to do that? If not, then I may as well tell you that you're only a dreamer. There's nothing wrong with being a dreamer, but a dreamer doesn't always get the results he wants. I know a lot of guys who dream but, without any discipline, they go nowhere. A person who gets results always executes from discipline. That, in my opinion, is everything, but it is overlooked by most.

Ability to Influence

The next key point is the ability to influence, teaching salesmen how to really listen to potential customers. The strategy includes the ability to influence and understand the needs of others. You're serving others and trying to build a relationship, not just trying to sell something to them.

I consider the word "sale" the same as the word "influence". It's not, "Make a sale, then I'm out." It's a human-to-human relationship that earns trust over time. Listen to the person. Find out what's going on in their lives. Find out what they need, what their goals are and what their dreams are. How you can service that? The ability to influence is understanding how to listen and then come up with solutions to help your customer.

When you are a sales leader, people watch every area of your business and if you don't do the simple disciplines necessary to get the results you want, you are not going to be able to influence many people. You want to be an example for others who will try to duplicate your efforts so that they can also succeed.

Success is fundamental. Even in basketball, they teach you how to make basic lay-ups and free throws first. They don't start you out with the long three-point shot or the fancy lay ups. The coaches focus on the simple fundamentals before they allow you to move on. As an intellectual salesman, your goal is to master the fundamentals which lead to success. It's not the fancy stuff, the marketing techniques or the way someone is so persuasive. It's the simple disciplines you learn that are going to become duplicatable. If you don't have them, your business success will reflect that.

Vision

One of the things I've learned is to try to mimic successful principles of discipline, ethics and focus and avoid the others. John Maxwell once wrote, "You can't lead from the middle. You have to lead from the top." So, as an intellectual salesman, I think you can be the leader even though you're not the one at the very top. Yet.

To close out this chapter, I'd like to reiterate the many characteristics of an intellectual salesman. Note that, even if a person doesn't have the full complement today, it's still possible for them to develop them over time.

Confidence in yourself and what you do. What you do makes a difference in people's lives.

Consistency and work ethic, or what you do every day.

Your ability to focus on any situation and your discipline with activities. Do you do the same disciplined acts even though you don't want to do them?

Your ability to listen. When you understand people's situations, it influences your ability to help them get to where they want to go.

Having consistent goals. What are your goals for that day or that month, that week, that quarter or that year?

Clarity

You must always be clear on what your goals are. You need to have goals in terms of what you want and need, not only on a yearly or quarterly basis, but also on a monthly and weekly basis. You can even drill down to a daily and hourly basis. If you're goal-oriented, find out what you need to achieve to get to those levels. If you can fully develop all these characteristics—confidence, consistency, focus, discipline, the ability to influence and goals—you'll be on pace for success in this industry.

3

MAJOR IN THE MAJORS

When I say "Major in the Majors," it's to help you understand how to balance your life in terms of your internal hierarchy of values. I don't know what other people call their majors but the ones for me are God, family, health and business, in that order.

I also believe that other majors include learning, loving, growing and serving on a daily basis. That has to be a focus every single day. I always ask people if they are excited. I mean, life is about being excited. Every week people say they hate Mondays and then they call Wednesday Hump Day and finally they Thank God it's Friday. Their most energetic time of their week is the weekends because that's when they get excited about life.

My belief is that you're supposed to live in a world where you're always excited for today. You're fortunate that you're alive and that you're able to enjoy. Without enthusiasm, there's nothing. If you're not excited about anything, what are you talking about? So, a lot of people ask me, what's a major? I think it's being excited about life. I think you should have a lot of energy and enthusiasm.

You never know how tomorrow's going to go. But one thing's for sure, there's never a day that's the same. The good thing is you can outline the day any way you want. Sometimes you'll meet a client who's going to challenge you. Sometimes you're going to meet a client who's going to get you upset. They may say something that may offend you so you have to learn how to handle your emotions. The ability to control your emotions is one of my favorite things. I try not to get too high or too low in any given situation.

Priority vs. Time

When it comes to illustrating how I manage my priorities, I'll use an example of rocks in a jar. You fill a jar up with sand and then try to stick big rocks in it. They won't fit. Your priorities are the big rocks and the question is, how many big rocks can you fit into a jar? It's priority management versus time management. With time management, my day is organized. Priority management is when my priorities are managed.

9:00am Rule

One of the ways I try to maintain a high level is to complete my major priorities by 9:00am so that, as the day progresses and a lot of little unexpected things come up, my priorities are not sidetracked. I think most people are great at time management but they're terrible at priority management. You must manage your priorities and your priorities must get done.

So in this jar example, you want to set the rocks and the big boulders in the jar first and then pour the sand in. That way the priorities have been handled. Not only that, water can be poured in with the sand because it fills in the gaps. At that point, you've got your priorities done. If you had stocked the jar with sand first, you wouldn't have been able to fit the rocks.

Your most important task, whether it's prospecting or marketing, is whatever is going to help you get the ultimate results. The goal is to try to get up by 6:00 in the morning, maybe get your meditation and exercising done, and then try to be in the office on time. That way you complete some of your most important tasks as early as possible so the rest of your day seems like you've accomplished much.

Many people don't accomplish anything during a workday except basic time management. They run a lot of errands, but they don't do anything priority-based that's going to get them the results that they want. To adhere to this rule, try to get things done as early as possible each day.

I realize that many of us need to commute a long distance but you can still fit some important items into that 9:00am rule. It could be just calling your assistant and making sure that she's helping you manage your priorities before you get into the office. Although it can be hectic on the road, it often becomes a time for me to just meditate. No phone, no nothing. Just get my mind in the right place. Sometimes I listen to some of the best motivational speakers or pastors while I'm driving to and from the office and utilize this as personal development time. For some people, it fuels them up to get ready to go.

Commuting time could be very productive versus sitting there listening to the Morning Zoo. Nothing wrong with listening to music because it is relaxing. All I'm asking is, does it serve you? I have nothing against whatever people do in the morning, as long as it's serving them to get the highest level of results. Always ask if this is serving you. No? Then eliminate it. Is watching the Kardashians serving you? Why does it serve you?

Sometimes, there's a built-in hurdle if you're dealing with other time zones. Say you're a sales person who deals with China, the Philippines, or Australia. How do you blend all that in to your schedule without tearing your day apart? Well, there has to be schedule. For me, if I'm dealing with our East Coast, I have to put it into my schedule for the day. I have agents in other states and other time zones and I do have to designate time for them but it's something that I'm scheduling ahead of time. I don't just wake up and make a call to them unless it's scheduled. I already know who I'm going to develop, who I'm going to follow up, and who I'm going to influence in other time zones. It's like anything else. You add it to your schedule and work accordingly.

Each salesman needs to make sure he's detailed in his schedule, make sure he's detailed in his life, and make sure he understands his goals for what he's going to achieve that day. By focusing on the 9:00am Rule, you can get your day going in the right direction. Here's a sample of how I keep a precise schedule of my daily activities.

My Daily Schedule

6:00 am   Wake Up

6:15 am   Exercise/Focus/Pray

7:00 am   Get Ready/Protein Drink/Greens

7:50 am   Commute

9:00 am   Review Email/Text

9:15 am   Client Strategy Meeting/Weekly Goals

9:40 am   Email/Coffee/Call Wife

10:00 am   Client Strategy Meeting

11:00 am   Projects/Presentations/Strategy/Planning

12:00 am   Conference Calls

12:30 pm   Lunch

1:00 pm   Phone (Money Time)

1:50 pm   Referral Sources

3:35 pm   Coffee/Call Wife/Children checkup

3:45 pm   Client Meeting

4:15 pm   Projects/Presentations/Strategy/Planning

5:30 pm   Commute

6:30 pm   Family Time/Gym/Play

7:00 pm   Family Dinner

8:45 pm   Family Time

11:00 pm   Personal Development/Schedule/Meditate/Pray

11:40 pm   Sleep

Exercise

When you work out, your body enjoys a natural high from the endorphins released. Lots of people find this enjoyable and this also helps boost your overall sense of well-being. Not to mention, working out is good for you.

You want to get your blood pumping and you want to stay healthy. You want to make sure you're thinking in the right frame of mind. I'm not saying you have to go to the gym and work out for three hours. I'm saying just take a walk outside or maybe do some basic calisthenics in the morning just to get your blood going and your mind thinking.

What's all this wealth for if you don't have your health? Exercise and eat right. Focus on the right diet plan. Always eat for fuel, not for taste. You know, I don't have a diet plan, I'm not a personal trainer or anything but I'm always trying to see how food is going to serve me. If I eat it and it makes me sleepy then that doesn't serve me. If I eat and have energy, that serves me. If I eat and I'm always getting sick, that doesn't serve me. If I eat and I never get sick then that's better for me.

Relax

Even if you can find only a half hour before bedtime to listen to relaxing music or curl up with a book, you'll find that it does wonders for your stress level.

Practice Empathy

While most people say they listen to others, they really don't listen with empathy. They listen to what they're going through, "Oh really, that sucks." But they don't feel what they're feeling. There's a big difference and I think you should feel what others are feeling to some degree so that you can understand the depths of what they're going through. Living with energy, enthusiasm, and empathy and in the balance of God, family, health and business, in that order, is what I believe makes a successful life.

4

METHODS VS. RESULTS

The perception is that successful people enjoy doing things that failures don't want to do. The reality is they do things that failures won't do despite the fact that they dislike doing them. Successful people form a habit of doing things that failures don't like to do.

Pleasurable methods vs. pleasurable results is one of my mantras. You may love to eat French fries and hamburgers because they taste great; it's a pleasurable task but the result is you're going to get out of shape or you're going to die if you eat too much of it.

So, what's better, a pleasurable method or a pleasurable result? In my opinion, it's the pleasurable result that matters most. Some things in moderation are fun, sure. But if you had fun 24 hours a day, you could also hurt yourself. It may be fun to visit Levi's Stadium to watch the 49ers play. But you can't go to the 49ers office every single day of the week wearing a 49ers jersey because you don't play for the team. You're just a fan and will get escorted out. It's a pleasurable method but it would not be a pleasurable result.

In business, the pleasurable methods include prospecting, presenting and following up. People don't want to do it. They hate it because it's not pleasurable. They want the results but they don't want to do the work to get them. People may love the sales side, but to become successful, there are going to be methods that aren't pleasurable. You may receive many rejections. You may hear a lot of people saying No. You may get your feelings hurt and think you're not succeeding. But you need to carry on and focus on pleasurable results, not pleasurable methods.

As a salesman becomes more successful, some of those not-so-pleasurable methods may actually become pleasurable. If you turned a situation like this into a habit, one you do often and become disciplined in, you'll start to love doing it. For example, I still enjoy having cheat days when I eat whatever I want. I used to cheat seven days a week but now I cheat only one. But I love the cheat day. I used to hate going to the gym but now I love it. I don't know if everybody truly loves to brush their teeth but they better do it!

This is also a good way for me to measure the growth of someone I'm mentoring. It's gratifying to see them start to do things that they once hated and turn them into strong and good habits. The ultimate test of a salesman's growth is to watch him do the things he hates to do first. He does them not because he has to, but because he wants to.

One of the things that I hated doing in the past was prospecting. I always had a challenge when I got in front of too many people. I just wanted to hang around and not say anything. I was scared because I felt that I didn't know enough to talk to so many different people. Deep inside, I was an introvert but then I said, "You know what? I'm just going to start talking to people." I eventually became a social butterfly. I had to convince myself that I do know enough in certain areas and I have also become a great listener so I can have a great conversation with anyone. In the old days, I was scared to be in a room full of people but today I love it. I used to be scared to speak in public. Now, I love talking to groups.

I couldn't imagine what my life would be if I retained my fear of public speaking because most of my career eventually developed around this skill. If I didn't overcome that one area of fear, I'd probably still be sitting in a cubicle and hating my job.It goes back to confidence. Build confidence as you develop your good habits, and you'll also develop the sense that you know what you know.

Become a Thermostat?

A thermometer measures the temperature of the body or the temperature of the room. But a thermostat is different because it regulates the temperature from cold to hot.

My question is, which one are you? Are you always measuring your business or are you setting the standards for it? Are you setting the culture for your business? Do you have high expectations or low expectations? Or do you have no expectations? You must want to create positive, excited expectations as you control the temperature of your life and your business. As a high producer, you want to be a thermostat and set your business on fire.

Just imagine if a thermometer and a thermostat were two different persons. Whom would you rather meet? The guy who sits around and says, "Whatever happens, happens. I guess whatever you tell me, that's what's going to happen." Or would you rather meet the guy who's the thermostat and sets the temperature? I know that person is going to set high expectations and I'd rather meet him.

Guiding Clients

Leadership is elevating someone to a higher place. Sometimes your client will ask himself, "Can I grow from this individual? Is this individual going to teach me?" To teach your customers, you need to set high expectations and standards because if you have low standards, there's no way to grow. How can you pull them to a higher place if you're not on higher ground? You must be on another level to set a higher standard for the client and anyone you are mentoring. A thermostat must set that by being at a higher level at all times.

Do most clients really know where they need to be? Is it a salesperson's job to be able to set that thermostat? Absolutely. I believe they are paying you and you are compensated for guiding a client in a direction best suited for them. For example, let's say you are in 24 Hour Fitness and you want to meet the fitness coach. I don't think the fitness coach should ask you, "So what kind of diet would you like?" He needs to set a high standard for you to follow. Whether you follow or not, it's up to you, but his role is to take you to another level based on his expertise.

It's the same with sales. When a person comes to meet one of our advisers to discuss retirement, I don't think they're meeting with us because they already have the answers. They're meeting with us because they know we have the answers and they want to hear what we can do for them.

I absolutely believe you must set that standard and guide your clients in the direction of their goals and needs. You have studied and become an expert so they trust you as a thermostat because of your knowledge, focus and commitment level.

5

STEPS TO SUCCESS

Right off the bat you want to have what I call 'realistic goals' and make them daily. You could say, "I want to be a millionaire this year", but if your daily goal is "do nothing", you're not going to be a millionaire. But if the daily goal is, "I am going to achieve _____ today" it becomes realistic for you to achieve on a consistent basis. Set realistic goals that are going to move you towards your ultimate goal. You could say your goal is to not go home today until you've confirmed three future appointments. OK, if you make three appointments every single day this week, that's great progress on a simple and very realistic goal.

Written Business Plan

Once you set that goal, put together a written plan for that goal. If you believe setting up three appointments a day is realistic for an eight-hour day, write that in your business plan. "OK, I'm going to do this every single day. If I do this, I should average X amount of sales. I should average X amount of clients to have this size of a client base."

See how that works out for the first week. Set realistic goals, then create a business plan based on your goals. No one else gives you these goals; they're your own. At the end of the week, it's easy for you to determine if you reached your goals.

Make Adjustments

Now let's make adjustments based on the results. What if, instead of locking in three appointments, you were able to get six? Awesome, right? Now your goals are, "I'm going to go for five or six because I was able to set up six consistently all week." But, what if it goes the other direction and you're only able to get one per day? One per day, believe it or not, is still extremely successful, but your goal was three so you need to make adjustments at the end of the week. An intellectual salesman is one who monitors his adjustments. Maybe you need to make forty calls to get your six appointments. Maybe you need to make fifty calls. Maybe you need to get more leads from your sources because you're running out of names.

Consistently Execute

Once you make adjustments and you see the consistent results, it then boils down to executing those numbers on a daily basis. When you do that consistently, you're going to get a ratio and be able to set a goal at the end of each week, month and year.

Create Accountability

From that point on, you want to be accountable to your goals. Some people need coaches, some need a person to monitor their activity, others have their own program where

THE INTELLECTUAL SALESMAN

they can base their progress on a point system. The more points I've accumulated, the better my week was. Everybody has their own systems and strategies, but you must create accountability, whether to yourself, to your team members, to your sales managers, or to your family. I don't care what your system is as long as you have something to track whether you're growing or not. Do that consistently in everything, whether it's success in your sales career, your faith or with your physical body.

Sometimes I'd like to have another set of eyeballs for my own accountability. I get down on myself if I don't hit my number and it would be great if someone could motivate me by giving me bigger goals. I have a mentor who gives me big goals but sometimes we need to stretch our vision. Sometimes working with a mentor who can spread your vision and help you stretch out will enhance what you can achieve.

Slow Erosion of Fundamentals

Over time, though, some salesmen begin to take their skills for granted. Once they establish a system that gets a result, they begin to cut corners because everything seems to be going along pretty well. They won't prospect as much or ask for referrals as often.

In sales, the more successful you become, the less desperate you want to appear. When you're a young, aggressive salesman, you don't mind the aggressive perception because you're just getting started. But then you get to a point of being somewhat successful. Maybe you've gone from making $50,000 a year to a quarter million a year. You might think, "Why do I need to call so many people when I'm making a quarter million or half million dollars a year? I'm not going to act like I need anything! I'm a prima donna! I'm at the highest level that I've ever been so why am I going to act like I need something from someone?"

Ego is one of the challenges of successful sales people. They start to believe their own clippings. They believe they're the best. They believe they're so great and now every client is lucky to have them. This all switches as they start to make money and, instead of being grateful for their clients, they take things for granted and begin the slow erosion of fundamentals.

One of the biggest things you can learn is to remain humble and hungry to serve others, regardless of the growth of your bank account. If you become a multi-millionaire after you started with nothing, don't treat clients as if you don't need them. No matter how big or small a client is, I'm just happy to have them. When a client says, "I will do business with you", whether big or small, it makes me feel fortunate and honored to represent them. Salesmen can't let their ego get in the way when they become successful. To maintain those results it's going to require the same fundamentals.

Sharpen your skills and get better. Never believe you've learned enough. Always work as if you're just getting started.

4 Basic Rules of Business

Rule #1: Say Please & Thank You

Always show polite gestures to your clients. Mean it, don't just say it. Whether it's a referral you're trying to get to, or the clients you want to serve, always say please and thank you.

Rule #2: Be Five Minutes Early

Clients appreciate you being early. I don't like people who are always late. I always try to be five minutes early on my appointments.

Rule #3: Finish What You Start

If you're going to start it, finish it. If you start it, get it done, no matter what. If you're on a path to go on a certain route, finish it. Get the results you're looking for. I think most people dabble in so many areas, they never become masters at anything. They've started many projects but have finished none. In this business, you're going to need to be focused and finish what you start.

Rule #4: Keep Your Promises

Do what you say you're going to do when you say you're going to do it. Be a person of integrity, one who keeps their word andtheir focus. I think many people make a lot of promises before a sale is made. But when the deal is done, the promises go out the window. You have to keep your promises even after the sale is made because that's when the work begins. Most people focus on the beginning of the sales process but keeping your promises after the sale always results in more business. Place the appropriate attention on the front end but also pay attention to the back end.Learn how to do follow-up, send thank you cards and create other habits that maintain a good relationship with the clients.

6

TAKE WHAT YOU DO SERIOUSLY

How serious are you about your daily schedule? When you work for yourself in sales, you always ask the question, "Who's your boss?" In reality, your boss is your schedule. Your schedule is the ultimate manager of your life and of your business because your schedule is your life.

Time is your life. It's what you manage on a daily basis. How you manage your time and how you manage your schedule will ultimately reveal the results of your business or your life. I look at each day based on the major priorities I'm trying to achieve that day that will give me a productive result.

I'm working in a world of high rejection. I love a business where the rejection is high. The lower the rejection, normally, the lower the income. So, that's why I'm always pursuing rejection.

If you look at a flight attendant, she's walking down the aisles asking if you want a drink. I guarantee you, if they received $1,000 for everyone who said yes to a drink, the flight attendant would be much more committed. She's going to ask you, "Are you thirsty?" "Are you sure you're not thirsty?" But because she doesn't make anything from that sale, she doesn't care if you get a drink or not. It doesn't affect her one bit because rejection is very low.

But if you're working on a multi-million dollar deal, you're dealing with a big client who has a lot of money; the rejection level is very high but the potential positive results are also very high. So, in creating priorities, I'm always trying to get high rejection, which will give me the highest reward for my time.

We all have all the same hours in a day but the key is for the higher producers to find out which parts of their day get them the highest results and which parts of the day get them the smallest results. Knowing that, they can focus on the high results and delegate the rest. So when you take what you do seriously, focus on the manager priorities and delegate everything else.

I was trained years ago that if you don't have an assistant, you are your assistant. That really affected me because I would find myself doing daily things that would produce very little results. Dry cleaning, getting my car washed, picking up my lunch, things that I could easily give someone else to handle. All those chores take time that I could use to focus on higher priorities. Taking what you do seriously includes paying attention to your time.

You must do what you hate most first in your day. You don't like to prospect? Do it first. You don't like to exercise? Do it in the morning.

When I say take what you do seriously, don't confuse business with production. I know a lot of people who are very busy all day but the production is very small. So, obviously, they're not focused on the right things.

It's all about the Customer

I do a lot of public speaking and a good friend of mine once asked, "How do you go on stage and not get nervous?" Whether you're on stage, whether you're with a client or one-on-one, it's the same. You always ask the question, "How do I serve?" not "How do I sell?" And every time you ask "How do you serve?" your whole feeling on stage changes. I'm just giving back, not looking for anything. And so, how you serve becomes the ultimate gift in closing.

Positive Business Image

One of my key points is to project a positive business image. I hate this side of it in terms of "perception is reality" because you can have a great person who is living out of means but he truly cares about his clients. But in the world that we're in, I think we've got to present a positive image of what we're offering. You should be utilizing the programs that you offer, which means if you're selling a certain car, you should own that car. If you're offering a certain type of copy machine, you should know how to use it. You should be a product of your product.

Now the image that you present is based on the perception you're trying to achieve. For example, if you're a rapper and you're selling your new album, your image is different from the image of someone who's offering a copy machine or a car. So you have to adapt based on theproduct that you're offering.

I was in the financial services retirement planning business, which required a professional image because that's what that generation is looking for. I can't come out looking like I'm offering something else. If I was working at a roller skate place, I think it'd be great to wear roller skates. Projecting a positive image is based on the product and services that you're offering, as long as it's appropriate.

In financial services, or retirement planning, I'm always on. I always assume I'm going to be walking in the mall one day and I may see a client who may have invested a million dollars with me. Do I want to look a certain way when I see them? The first thing you've got to ask yourself is, are you representing who you are? That means do you feel that what you're representing becomes a part of you.

In sales, passion is when you love what you do so much that you would do it for free. Would you do this if you made no money? If that's the case, do you enjoy life? For me, I enjoy dressing up. I enjoy looking sharp. I enjoy giving an impression that makes me feel good, not to impress the world but to create an image based on whatever product or services I'm selling.

Know your Customers

This is of the ultimate importance because you need to know what your customer wants and needs so that they'll know they can buy it from you. If you don't know what they want, if you can't seem to find a way to serve them, they'll never buy from you. They're going to be able to be read you very easily. "You're just about the money, you're just about you, you're just about trying to close me to pay rent or to pay for your groceries." A client can feel the desperation. So you need to know your customer well. Study your client's goals, needs, and objectives and then reach your goal to service them.

Become Known as an Expert

The more you feed yourself, the more inclined you will be to becoming an expert. If you're offering a certain program, your goal is to be an expert in that program. I could ask anyone, if they were going to purchase a product or service from anyone, would they look for an expert or an amateur on that product? If the answer is they want someone to be an expert, then you better learn your craft. You should build and devote enough time for you to be an expert in your craft. If you don't, are you sure you're hungry enough for this? Maybe you're in the wrong industry.

I would say 10,000 hours is still the magic number to be an expert in something but I don't think you put a time limit on passion. If you take every moment in life as a growing and learning experience, life is a wonderful journey of growth because you're learning from it every single day.

I've seen plenty of data to support the idea that you can make $100 an hour or more simply by specializing in an area you already know. If you are a doctor, you can develop a specific area of expertise and teach it to others in your field. A plumber or an architect or an accountant can do the same.

Not every skill lends itself to this kind of opportunity but you'd probably be surprised to discover how many lines of work can. I know one guy who makes $150,000 a year teaching martial arts instructors how to do a better job with their studios. Another friend of mine makes a six-figure income helping direct marketers find inexpensive premiums. A neighbor of mine teaches car salesmen how to sell more cars. And there are hundreds of former restaurateurs out there teaching fledgling restaurateurs what they know about that business.

You can work for a salary for the rest of your life and grow wealthy slowly or you can become a consultant in your field, make at least as much money as you do now, and work a lot less. You can do this if you know how.

- Develop your own newsletter

- Get articles published in trade magazines

- Get invited to shows and seminars

- Write and publish books

- Take advantage of public relations

Becoming a freelance expert is something you can do now or later. But if you think it's something that would interest you—if you like the idea of working part-time from your home for good money—you should start the process now. Why now? Because to become a well-paid consultant you have to specialize. Nobody's going to pay a generalist $100 an hour.

You can specialize. You can develop top-notch expertise in some special area of your industry. You can do that and you can learn how to sell yourself. But all that will take a little time. And that's why you need to start now, so that you can make the transition sometime next year when you're ready. Once you are confident that you know as much about your specialty as does anybody in the business, you'll be able to sell yourself with confidence.

Think about your line of work. Who gets paid the most? What kinds of problems cause the most trouble? What kind of opportunities result in the greatest profits?

Answering questions like these will help you choose a specialty that will get you the hourly rate that you want. Developing a reputation as an expert in your industry can raise your business's profile, help you attract customers, partners and employees and even enable you to charge more for your products and services. You're already an expert in what you do and spreading the word about that expertise is easier than you might think. Here are 10 tips to get you started.

Give a speech

Find organizations that your target customers belong to— the local marathon runners' training group, PTA or Rotary club—and offer to speak at their meetings.Create a relevant handout to leave behind and bring business cards and brochures, too.

Start a blog

Adding a blog to your business website is a smart tactic for companies that provide information and expertise, such as accounting or consulting firms. Blog about industry news, timely advice for your customers, or new developments in your business.

Comment on other blogs

If you don't have the time or skill to blog, build your reputation by commenting on your industry's leading blogs.

Make sure your comments are thoughtful and add to the conversation. Don't be overly promotional, but do include your name and business name.

Use Twitter

Use Twitter not just to promote your business, but also to share interesting links and re-tweet useful information. Focus on quality, not quantity. By consistently sharing good information, you'll build a reputation as a knowledgeable source.

Join LinkedIn

If you own a business-to-business company, LinkedIn Groups and Answers are great ways to share your expertise. Join Groups related to your industry and participate in discussions. Look for LinkedIn Questions related to your business and answer them.

Write articles

Blogs and online publications are influential, but print media still carries more weight with most people. Contact trade publications and local newspapers and ask if you can contribute articles related to your industry or even write a regular column.

Become a trusted source

Being quoted in print or online cements your reputation as an expert. Seek out journalists who cover your industry, then make yourself a resource by commenting on their articles and sending them information related to their "beat"...and your business.

Lead the way

To become an industry expert, you've got to be active in your industry. But don't just attend industry events and conferences. Take a leadership role by offering to head committees, speak at events or develop programs.

Network

Be an active networker, both online and offline. Focus not on what you can gain, but on how you can help others by connecting them and sharing valuable information. People will come to view you as a reliable and trustworthy resource.

Get involved in your community

Keep a high profile in your community by participating in local events. For instance, if you own a health club, you could sponsor a fitness fair or get a booth. The more active you are in your community, the more business will come your way.

Invest in yourself

I always recommend reading a book a week, if you can. If you can't, listen to books in your car. With today's technology, you have an unlimited amount of online information and you can download a lot of it for free. The question is, do you feed yourself? Because most people stop learning when they graduate from college. They believe they've learned enough and think they're OK. That's dangerous in terms of your career. I mean, look at it just from the perspective of computer technology. If you graduated in the late 80s or 90s with a computer degree, what is the value of that information in 2014? None at all. There is no value in learning MS-DOS or those programs that were around back then. If you don't keep up with that type of technology, you're a dinosaur. You don't want to be a dinosaur in your industry or your own business so adopt good personal development habits; strengthen your ability to grow and create excellence in your own life and business.

Be Accessible

You've got have a daily schedule to return phone calls and emails at a scheduled time. You should have your phone on silent during the day and only at certain times should you look for calls that need to be returned. If you're always available, how do you focus if everyone needs you at different times of the day? In the evening, my phone is off. In the morning, it goes back to a detailed schedule.

I'm not a reactor, okay? I'm a person who works on a schedule so that I don't stress. So, are there certain things that could break a schedule? Sure. Emergencies, my daughter gets sick or needs to be picked up from school. There are ways to find me. But in terms of the daily schedule, make it so that you're proactive, not reactive.

Build a Rock-solid Reputation

When you're young and you're moving up in sales, the most important thing is getting results. But as you start to age and mature, you start to realize integrity and character matters even more than getting the job done. I think some people compromise integrity to get numbers or money or results.

I think if your "always goal" is to do the right thing for people and do the right thing for customers, you'll earn a great reputation because you always have good intention. I know there are people out there who are great sales people but their only intention is to close ten customers. The customer will also feel that.

But as you start to mature in your career, you establish integrity and care about people more, and then your reputation follows you. If you take advantage of people and all you care about is your numbers, trust me, your reputation will also reflect that. No one's going to want to go to you. You'll just notice it because no one will call you, no one will offer business to you, no one will be seen walking into your office because of your reputation. Integrity and character play the biggest parts of this whole process because, without the right intention, you won't succeed.

Get Involved

You want to get to the point of immersion. Getting involved means that your business becomes part of you, part of your culture and how you work on a daily basis. Influence is when people see your passion in the way that you work and communicate. When I see someone great at what they do, it really attracts me. It could be anything, a person singing, a person playing the piano. When I see a person who is truly passionate about what they do, it influences me big time and that matters. That's why we're out here.

Follow-up Constantly

Most of the time you're either presenting or prospecting to meet people or to get referrals. You're presenting your service to someone or you're following up to get more appointments to grow your business. Constant follow-up is important. It includesdeveloping referral sources who, even if they can't do business with you, will refer others who can. Follow-up is understanding your marketing strategy to get you in front of more people. When I say follow up consistently, I mean, "Are you growing your business consistently?" Are you trying to get in front of more people consistently?

Prospecting, presenting and follow-up are the three keys to sales success. Following up with your prospects, following up with one of your referrals, following up with your clients, and following up with whatever marketing strategy you have. You must follow up with your business on a daily basis and know where you are every single day.

7

SOCIAL MEDIA

The challenge for traditional sales is there are many guys who are old school. They only use a prospect list, calling them one at a time. That guy is being laughed at because we're in the day of social media and his competition is able to take advantage of technologies the old guy doesn't understand. I've seen and trained many sales people who've mastered social media and talk to hundreds, if not thousands, at a time. The old school salesmen need to learn how to use modern resources to once again become experts in their field.

One of the distractions I mentioned was emails and texts and tweets and all that social media kind of stuff. It is a different world for sales people and it begs the question, "Is there an upside to social media for the modern sales person?"

The answer is, absolutely yes. I believe social media has its place in sales. This is a good way to endorse or brand yourself. Traditionally, you'd need to purchase expensive advertising, maybe commercials or television or billboards, to get your name out there. With YouTube, Facebook and Twitter, you can get your name out where a lot of people can see it. You could have thousand of friends who are able to see your work on a daily basis. I think it definitely has its advantages.

Social Networking to Promote Your Business

The goal of business owners is to make money. However, to sell your product or service you need to alert the general public. That is why you need to advertise your business.

Fortunately, not all forms of advertising cost money. There are ways to promote the products or services that you sell without having to spend any money at all.

One of the ways is by using an online social networking website. Millions of regular Internet users belong to at least one social networking website but social networking is also used by businesses. In fact, that was originally how social networking got started.

These websites allow you to share your business information with other business owners and to develop close relationships with those who share an interest with you. Essentially, this means that you can develop valuable business information and possibly walk away with a new business partner or client.

The Power of Social Media

Social media sites include Facebook, Twitter, LinkedIn, Google + and Pinterest. These types of sites all have one thing in common and that is sharing information. If a person enjoys a photo, video or an article they will share it with their friends. This could have a massive viral effect and a huge impact on your business.

Make a great video about your business and post it on Facebook. One person shares it on their page and his friends may share that link. Before long, one person has showcased your product to hundreds or thousands of people. Now that's good for business!

This is the potential power social media sites hold today and the number one reason why so many businesses use a Facebook Page.

How to Utilize Social Media for Your Offline Business

By incorporating social media sites into your offline business you are able to stay in touch with your customers any time of the day. Whether you offer products or a service, you can use social media sites effectively. By posting updates to your pages you are keeping in contact with your customers and potentially reaching new ones.

With Facebook, for example, you can post special deals or coupons. When you introduce a new product, write about it and share a photo. People who have liked your page may take advantage of the special offer.

Twitter is great for sending out short messages which can be extremely effective. If you are a restaurant owner, you can send out a message at 5pm and offer a dinner special to attract people into your restaurant.

Help I'm Confused

There are consultants who specialize in setting up and promoting social media for offline businesses. They are experienced in setting up business pages, getting people to

Like, Follow or Friend you. Plus they know how to increase your exposure with effective marketing tactics such as getting other business owners to send you traffic.

Hiring a Social Media Consultant can be a huge time saver but, as with anything new, expect a learning curve. If you don't have the time or energy to do this but understand the importance of using these sites, this is a fantastic way to go.

The Benefits of Using Social Media Sites

- Potential to reach hundreds if not thousands of new people
- Allows people to comment on a new product after using it
- Provides a way for you to interact and follow up with your customers/clients
- Creates interaction with people uploading stories, images and experiences
- Can be used as an additional marketing platform

Imagine if you owned a kitchen supply store. You could get your customers to post pictures of meals that they have prepared using your supplies. They could even post recipes and share baking tips and stories. In between all of these posts you can inject your own tips, along with useful products and discount coupons. This is what helps create repeat customers.

Social media sites are a way to share important details with your customer base outside of the traditional business setting. As customers become more interactive they will automatically share their experiences with their friends, which in turn will increase your customer base and your profits.

When using social media be cautious. I see people posting pictures of their food, posting pictures of their clothes or posting pictures of things that may not be prudent; people won't want to buy anything from that person. While social media may be a great way to advertise who you are, what you do and what you represent, it's also a way to show too much of who you are, show too much of what's going on and open you up for negative perception.

I don't know if this is a derogatory statement, but poor social media habits could drop you into the collection bin of the middle class.

Not to be mean, but let's say you're trying to reach the highest level in business. Well, ask yourself if the highest level of executives post on Facebook. Do you see Donald Trump posting pictures of his family, of barbeques, or trips to baseball games? Do you see the presidents of the largest Fortune 500 companies, or the best sales people in the world, out there on social media saying, "Oh, I'm eating my food today"? If you want to be average, then let everyone see everything you do.

New Breed

Silicon Valley has created a whole different type of sales mentality from the Philip Morris days of the 60's, 70's and 80's and that has resulted in a different breed of salesman.

You have to be a lot more technically savvy to survive in today's world. There are products that you can sell by utilizing the same talents as before. But Silicon Valley changes the way we do business. So I think you should able to keep up in certain areas. Do I believe there's still a place for people to sell certain programs the old fashioned way? Sure. But the ones who use the Internet can sell more and sell faster. You don't want to be a dinosaur in 2015. The web makes things faster so you've got to be sharper and more detail-oriented while, at the same time, remaining influential.

Now that we are now global economy, it adds another layer to the sales mix. You are not limited to only certain geographical areas anymore. On the web, you can sell the same product around the world and you see a lot of people doing just that. Sales people aren't just selling basketball shoes in Boston and San Francisco because TV, radio and the Internet has made NBA a global league. The players themselves are able to tweet themselves to millions of followers worldwide. So with the ability to have followers around the world, you should be able to shout out your message and hear what the market is clamoring for. You now have the ability to offer products nationwide or internationally and have an influence because of the number of people you can reach.

In a global economy, that requires new language skills and the ability to deal with somebody who's not in your own backyard. If I'm training somebody with a lot of potential, just coming out of college, and they ask how to be the best sales person they could possibly be, I have the answer.

8

STRESS

Stressed salesmen often act like zombies. You'll notice that they don't sleep very well and they're often angry. They may be sitting at the dinner table with their children but they're on the phone the whole time. They're probably also looking at emails or texting while their family looks on. The reason is they never took time management seriously and now they can't turn their job off.

If you're going to take this career seriously, you need to balance your life well enough to eliminate stress, one of the biggest killers of salesmen. If your goals are set properly, you willeliminate stress. The best way for me to eliminate my stress is by having my day plan already written out. When I know how my day looks like from beginning to the end and I know what I've accomplished and the priorities I've set, I sleep better. So, take what you do seriously, watch your priorities, watch your scheduling and take a day very seriously because each day is a gift and there's no guarantee of tomorrow.

You need to take a serious approach to reducing stress. Start by figuring out what is stressing you out, and how you're currently dealing with it. Then remove the stressful triggers you can control. For the times you can't avoid stress, you must find constructive ways to deal with it. You cannot perform at your peak when you are under stress. If you want to say hello to success, then say goodbye to stress.

In order to understand the true sources of your stress, it helps to examine your natural excuses, habits, and attitudes that crop up when you're exposed to stress. For example, when faced with stress, do you have a tendency to explain it away as a "temporary" state, even though you can't remember the last time you really took a break and stepped away from your work? Do you explain it away as part of your normal behavior ("I'm highstrung") or just as a natural part of life ("My life is always busy and crazy")?

These are common ways that individuals try to explain away their stress. The problem with these coping mechanisms is that they minimize the problems. All they do is put your stress on the back burner and put you in a position of permanently being out of control with your reactions to tough situations.

The truth of the matter is that you are in control. Identify your stress sources and then take active steps toward dealing with them in a more responsible, proactive manner and you'll be much happier.

Burnout

Many people who experience constant stress are actually experiencing a form of burnout. It occurs most often in people who feel as though they are always under the gun and are unable to meet expectations. It can end up sapping your productivity and your energy and you might feel helpless, hopeless, and very resentful.

What are the signs of burnout? The biggest one, of course, is constantstress and having no ways to work into a positive channel. Other signs of burnout may include:

- Feeling as though every day is a bad one

- Being constantly exhausted

- Your day is spent either in mind-numbing tasks or being completely overwhelmed

- You feel as though all of your efforts go unappreciated

- It seems like too much effort to care about your work or your personal life

People who are going through burnout tend to disengage completely, having lost their motivation to work and being consumed by hopelessness. What makes burnout even more insidious is that many people don't even realize that they're going through it.

Who is at risk for burnout? Essentially anybody who feels overworked and undervalued. The most important thing to cultivate in order to prevent burnout is a strong support system. Of course, the process is personal and different for every person. But in an overarching sense, we've compiled a list of directives that may help you figure out what causes you stress and how you can remove yourself from stressful situations.

Avoid people who stress you out—Good friends make you feel better and create a relaxing or a fun environment in which to unwind. Most people, however, have a couple of "friends" who generally end up causing more stress than they relieve. This doesn't mean that anybody who's having an off day is a bad friend and you need to cut all ties, but consider how much stress certain relationships cause you.

Control your living environment—If the news makes you stressed out, don't watch it. If your commute traffic causes you stress, take an alternate route.Even if it takes longer, the lack of a headache is worth the detour.

Learn how to say No—It's OK to say No every once in a while. If they appreciate your work, they'll understand and give you the space that you need.

There are plenty of things you can do to shift the elements in a stressful situation to help you cope better and feel less stressed.

Try to compromise—In the event that your stress is due to the behavior of someone else, it can often help to engage them in a frank and firm discussion about why you find the situation so stressful. You might be surprised at what you learn about the other person, as well. Compromise is the key to success!

Be assertive—Many people find that they experience less stress and lead happier lives when they take control of the situations that cause them stress and meet the challenges head on. Tell people if you are unhappy.

Manage your time and assets better—Planning will do more for you than you ever thought possible. Don't wait until the last minute to do things; this causes stress to build.

What many people neglect to consider is how they care for their bodies. Stress is a natural response, and if you are working with a healthy body to start off with, your response to stress will be much better than if you are living an unhealthy lifestyle. Staying fit and eating right can make a bigger difference than you'd ever considered. With this in mind, consider these tips when trying to change your lifestyle and deal with stress.

Exercise regularly—We always make it our New Year's resolution to work out more, but few actually follow through on their claims. This is a shamebecause, not only does working out make you look and feel good, it's a key element in helping your body deal with stressful situations. You don't even have to be a marathon runner to reap the benefits—just get a little bit of aerobic exercise, thirty minutes three times a week. It can make a big difference in your health and stress levels.

Eat healthy—If your body is fueled properly, it will run better and you'll be better able to deal with whatever the day throws your way. Always remember to eat breakfast—it really is the most important meal of the day. Your trials and tribulations will seem much worse if you start the day with your tank empty.

Reduce sugar and caffeine—This doesn't mean that you have to deny yourself your daily cup of Joe or swear off donuts forever, but if you make an effort to reduce your consumption of these products, your blood sugar levels will remain more constant and you'll feel better.

Get enough sleep—Your mother wasn't lying when she talked about beauty sleep. In this case, though, the beauty is definitely more than skin deep. Getting enough sleep fuels your mind as well as your looks.

9

FEAR

Fear and uncertainty are a salesman's worst enemies. When I began sales, I was always scared to ask the customer to buy. It's understandable for you to fear the word "No" but don't be discouraged.

Fear of rejection comes from human insecurity. Remember back in school you had to wear the right clothes if you wanted to fit in? The reason you didn't wear pink tube socks with green velvet jackets was because of the fear of rejection. No one wants to feel rejected in any form. It makes us feel bad about ourselves. By reading this book, you will learn to love rejection.

When you face your worst fears, you realize how they're holding you back. Opportunities simply pass you by when you're so afraid of doing something that you do nothing. It may be opportunities with people, situations or personal growth that can be yours when you learn to work through the resistance that fears cause.

Extreme fears can also cause insecurities that will haunt you day and night until you learn to cope with them. It can cause loss of self-esteem, which can lead to depression, isolation and other problems that can sabotage your life.

After you've identified and faced your most destructive fears, it's time to develop strategies for moving forward. It may be interesting to note that your subconscious brain doesn't recognize the difference between reality and your imagination. Here are some other ways that fear can impair you:

Destructive behaviors are a result of your fears. If you've experienced procrastination, neglect even the most basic of responsibilities, and doubt yourself at every turn, you probably have a fear linked to success. That fear of change and being unworthy or unprepared can hurl you into a tailspin.

Intellectual, emotional and decision-making abilities are sometimes impaired by fear because it won't let you move outside of your comfort zone and experience new ways of doing and thinking. You'll never live life fully if you can't open yourself up to challenges that can help you grow. Since fear is usually irrational, you won't make good decisions if you let the fear tie you down and narrow your perspective of a situation.

Fear isn't all bad. It can be a touchstone to make real and positive changes in your life. What has caused debilitating loss of energy and a rollercoaster of emotions in the past can actually become perfect opportunities for growth and progress.

Motivation is what keeps us going, searching, learning and taking chances. When you identify and face the fears that keep you from being motivated, you'll remove the obstacle that keeps you from full enjoyment of life. You can condition yourself to turn futile thoughts to hopes for the future.

Defeating Your Worst Fears

You don't have to be afraid of fear anymore. No matter what your fears, there are ways to cope with them. Here are a few strategies that help to deal with fear:

Build your self-esteem—When you think highly enough of yourself, there's hardly anything that will get you down permanently. Whatever fear you're harboring will become dimmer in nature when you know you have the ability to cope with any problem.

Interrogate yourself—After you've identified and isolated your worst fears, ask yourself a series of questions to help understand them more. Questions such as, "What's the worst that can happen?" and "What can I do to minimize the fear?" are good questions to pare down the fear to a manageable size.

Do what you're afraid of—If you're afraid of heights, climb a mountain; if you're afraid of sharks, swim with them. That's also true about what we fear in our everyday lives. If you're afraid of public speaking, join a Toastmaster's club. Doing what you're most afraid of will make you feel more capable and less frightened.

Use visualization—Olympic contenders often use visualization techniques to help them exceed their limitations. Visualization can help you overcome fear by imagining how you cope with the fear before it becomes a reality.

Take small steps—Fear can feel like an ominous cloud hovering over your life. You can't wipe out years of fear in a day. It will take time and strategy to convince your subconscious that you're not afraid of whatever is holding you back from experiencing life to the fullest.

Relax—Learn how to relax by reading books, taking a class or speaking with a counselor. When you learn how to relax your mind, you'll also learn how to turn your thoughts into less fearful ones.

Take control of your life—Fearful people are usually pessimistic and that powerful force of fear can be like a huge boulder on your back. When you confront your fears and take back control, you'll likely be surprised that the worst you thought could happen doesn't.

Exploring the origins of your fears may help you to overcome the ones you now face. For example, if you had parents who were negative in their language patterns, you may have grown up thinking, "I can't..." and may still be afraid that you won't be able to do certain things.

If fear in any form is holding you back from developing key skills that could help you reach an ultimate goal in life, you owe it to yourself to explore that fear and take steps to deal with them successfully.

It will take work and time, but you can rid yourself of these annoying and sabotaging fears and become the person you were meant to be.

10

HOME / WORK BALANCE

I work where I can constantly see my family around. You'll notice pictures around me when I work. It gives me a vision board of my family and shows me why I do this.

When I say workspace, it's not just office workspace, it's general life workspace. For an entrepreneur, their whole life is a workspace. For example, do you get up earlier? Do you exercise in the morning? That's part of your workspace. When you exercise and clear your mind and meditate, you get to work clear of issues. Also, when you get off work, you schedule to spend time with your family.

I think one of the worries for most people in this industry is that they're working almost from the time they wake up to when they go to sleep. They don't ever get a chance to just turn off and zone out. I think that zoning out is so critical.

Workspace is also your mental capacity to handle things in life. Yes, you could work all day but does it serve you? Are you exhausted the following day? Or, you could work all seven days but are you already tired on Monday morning? I don't do any work on Sunday. It's my time for family and God, to focus and get my head straight so that on Monday I'm fresh.

So, workspace is not just your office. It's the space that comes by creating a life that is manageable for you to enjoy the best results.

Get and Stay Organized

Sometimes I put too much on my calendar but my assistant will look at it and say, "Hey, you're overwhelmed." The issue there is delegation, taking on too much and overdoing it. Now, don't get me wrong, some people don't do enough but there could be a moment when you're working so much that your schedule is not allowing you to give the client your best.

Sometimes I fill out a lot of applications to do a presentation for someone and it's mentally draining. When you're sitting with someone and you're explaining certain concepts or services you become mentally exhausted even after an hour or two. I used to do back-to-back-to-back sessions but now I put gaps inbetween so I can allow my mind to relax. Don't forget, delegating areas of your life will help balance your time.

Working at home comes with lots of benefits, but it's important to have an effective organizational plan to make it profitable. These strategies for organizing your workday and environment will help you meet your goals.

Strategies for Organizing Your Workday

Set a starting time—Punctuality counts even when you report to yourself. Determine a realistic time when you can be ready to get down to business each morning.

Give yourself a quitting time—Hold onto your leisure and family time. It's just as important to establish an end to your workday.

Leave room for breaks—Give yourself a chance to take a breather.

Put your daily calendar in writing—Organize your tasks and meetings into a daily calendar.

Keep regular sleep hours—You need a full night's sleep to be at your best.

Evaluate yourself—Give yourself a monthly review to identify helpful improvements.

Strategies for Organizing Your Environment

Designate a specific work area—Having a home office devoted exclusively to business makes it easier to focus on professional activities.

Minimize interruptions—Let family and friends know the best time to contact you on workdays. Post a reminder on your office door during conference calls or when you need to avoid disturbances.

Limit visitors and errands—It's nice to be helpful and hospitable but ensure your day remains manageable.

Call in expert help—Browse online for forums geared to your situation or book aconsultation with a professional organizer.

Keep Work at Bay While on Vacation

Like any other hardworking professional, you deserve to enjoy your downtime away from the corporate world. Being committed to excellence is certainly admirable but everyone needs downtime away from work-related activities. Your family deserves time without dueling for your attention.

If you have a vacation on the horizon, make the conscious decision to separate your vacation time from your professional pursuits. You deserve the time off, and you'll return to work with a fresh perspective and renewed energy if you do.

Close all communication—Turn off your cell phone and refrain from checking email while on vacation. The messages will still be there when you get back. If you're concerned about missing calls from family members and friends, purchase a prepaid cell phone specifically for your trip or give them the hotel's phone number.

Set boundaries—Make clear boundaries to protect your privacy throughout your vacation. Tell your employer and coworkers that you're devoting 100% of your time to your family and prefer to only be contacted in case of an emergency.

Tie up loose ends—The month before your vacation, tie up all loose ends on outstanding projects. Get a head start on any deadlines that are looming shortly after your return to the office.

Answer questions—Before you leave for vacation, have a meeting with your boss. Answer questions he has about what needs to be accomplished while you're absent.

You've worked all year to earn your vacation time. Live in the moment and enjoy the time with your loved ones. No matter what happens at the office, it can wait until you return. Return to work rejuvenated and excited instead of feeling like you spent your whole vacation working. You deserve the rest. Enjoy it!

11

TEAM BUILDING

In my opinion, team building is one of most rewarding skills you can have as a sales professional. Building others is helping sales professionals become strong from the inside out. In a sales career you will encounter so many different emotions. Some months you will feel as if you can close anyone, but some months you will feel that you cannot close anything! One of the most rewarding things to witness is to see a new salesman become successful by utilizing the tools and strategies you were able to transfer to them.

As a team builder or trainer, you must know the difference betweenbuilding and motivating. Most sales trainers focus on motivation without building. You can have the most motivated person but he can still be unproductive. You must instill the Intellectual Sales professional ethic to truly build a consistently strong producer.

Builders focus on emotional control, follow-through, commitment, knowledge of product, homework, client needs and objectivesand presentation.

Motivational leaders focus on many things also, including passion, fear, supply and demand, greed, need, competition, winning, being #1, and being the best. Your goal is to be a leader who creates TEAMWORK through building and motivation!

Teamwork is drilled into us at an early age. We join Little League or work with other kids to complete school projects. We are encouraged to be a team member and to get along with the rest of the players.

As we grew into adults, we continue to collaborate to get work done and help a business grow. Collaboration is a big key for any small business as sharing important tasks leads to achieving shared goals.

You must communicate what you expect from the team but make sure they know that collaboration is only a minimum standard in your business. Team members should keep communication lines open because miscommunication creates hard feelings that can undermine the team's success. Each member should make a concerted effort to be understood and heard.

Your team should have goals to work toward on a quarterly or other regular basis. Having the team focus on these goals keeps each member's efforts aligned with the desired outcome. You can always re-evaluate the goals if needed.

Encourage a creative atmosphere where team members can question and brainstorm without judgment. Nurture a can-do attitude.

Leverage team member strengths by putting each member in a position for success.

Teams should learn to build trust with one another. They should be honest in their dealings and learn how to eliminate conflicts of interest.

Team members come from diverse walks of life with different perspectives and backgrounds. They should be encouraged to get to know each other well. Every idea should be based on its own merits, not the individual suggesting it. Encourage team members to learn from one another.

Team leaders and managers are responsible for informing team members about the role they play and what is expected of them. When the company has a positive and well-functioning collaborative team the business runs smoother and people are happier in their jobs.

Strengthen Your People Management Skills

People management skills are important in all walks of life. Strengthening these skills can help you live the life you desire.

Imagine how much easier life would be if people heeded your every wish. Your business life would soar to new heights. Strong people management skills can make all this possible.

You can gain these people skills by becoming familiar with some basic psychology and then putting this knowledge to work for you. We all share some basic desires. We all have many of the same wants and needs. When you meet the needs of other people, they tend to be easier to get along with. With patience, practice, and a willingness to understand people, you can develop strong management skills. Here are some good techniques for strengthening your people management skills:

Put yourself in their shoes—If you had their position, would you like yourself as a manager? Great managers know what people are thinking and feeling. They're quick to pick up on things and work hard to solve problems among their team. Ask yourself if you're willing to do the same.

Show gratitude and appreciation—You might feel appreciative of your team, but without action they'll never know it. Always be on the lookout for new and exciting ways to show these emotions.

Remember to say Thank you—People love to be appreciated and a sincere "Thank you" makes them feel good. Show your appreciation by doing special things for others that you know they'll appreciate.

Give sincere compliments—Think about what you really like about your team and point these things out as compliments. If you're sincere, chances are that the recipient will sense your genuine appreciation.

Respect—Strive to always treat people with respect, no matter their stance in life. Treat them the way you'd like to be treated. This shows character and strength, both of which are characteristics of someone with superior people skills.

Delegate appropriately—When you delegate the right tasks to the right people, everyone gets a chance to excel and the team works together at its best.

Be honest—If you've ever been caught in a lie, you know how quickly you can lose someone's trust. Earning and maintaining trust is an important people management skill. When others trust you, they believe in you, and your opinions mean more to them.

Listen attentively—Listening is fifty percent of communication. Make an effort to understand their point of view, even if you don't agree with it. When they know you consider their feelings important, you've already won half the battle. Practice these strategies each day in your communications with others, and one day soon you'll find that more and more people agree with you!

Reward Motivated Employees

You have probably worked for someone who refused to acknowledge or reward your work. You know, that boss who expects you to work around the clock for minimal pay, who discourages his employees from creating friendships, asks you to work on projects that are below your level and often tells other employees how he doesn't like you or your work. He made your job miserable and you couldn't wait to find a new one.

On the other hand, you have team members who are very motivated and perform well. If your key employees are motivated to put in the time and extra effort to do a good job on a project they should be rewarded. Rewards don't always need be financial. There are many ways to make employees feel rewarded for their hard work.

Money—This includes bonuses, raises, stock options and other financial gains.

Recognition—People like being thanked for doing their job.

Opportunity—Offer a new opportunity to join a high level board, to further their education or enjoy a mentorship.

Lunch—Invite them to an exclusive meeting with a key client.

Flex Time—Allow them to work from their home one or two days a week or let them start and end their days earlier.

Time off—Give them a comp day or extra time for lunch.

Rewarding your team members for their hard work can keep them motivated. They will appreciate your caring and continue doing a good job for you. Rewards don't have to cost your business a lot of money if they're personalized to fit their needs and goals.

Minimizing Conflict

As a team leader, you need to be prepared to resolve and minimize disputes when they crop up. Encourage your team members to take part in the development phase of the project. Make sure you put all commitments and expectations in writing and monitor work in progress frequently so you can identify and resolve any small conflicts before they become huge issues. This can include holding regular status meetings with your team where you can get updates on the project as well as any concerns.

Open a clear line of communication. Team members should articulate their ideas clearly. Communicate clearly and openly about priorities and goals of the project.

Everyone should be encouraged to ask questions, get clarification or paraphrasing for whatever they don't understand.

The team leader should be available so the members can express their issues immediately.

Encourage team members to keep conflicts professional. They should stick to facts and issues not personalities.

Encourage different points of view and be honest when expressing views.

Have team members focus on solutions when they have conflicts.

Anticipate possible problems before they arise.

Before you assign members to your team for the project, explain your communication principles.

Keep it clear that all team members have access to team leaders, management and supervisors. They should know that their opinions and perspectives are of value to the business.

Encourage mutual respect among all members of your team as well as those they are working for.

If Conflict Occurs:

As the team leader or manager of a project or group you need to be prepared for conflicts to happen at any time. Every business has some form of conflict among their employees. The main thing is to take steps to minimize as much as you can before it happens.

Listen to all sides of the story. Study body language, tone of voice and the demeanor of everyone involved.

Acknowledge the issue and their concerns.

Be proactive. Deal with the problem quickly and make it clear the ultimate goal is a successful project.

12

LEADERSHIP

You may be surprised to know that it takes a good follower to be a great leader. Everyone has a boss, whether it's a supervisor in a factory, a CEO of a Fortune 500 company, or the President of the United States. Here are some of the qualities of a good follower that make for great leaders:

Humility—Just as followers don't brag or become grandiose about their accomplishments, great leaders should also be humble. Shining the spotlight on others makes them look good and you look even better.

Clear about their roles—Both leaders and followers are clear about what role they play in the scheme of things.

Obedience—A follower who portrays a good role model for others by being obedient to the boss demonstrates a good organization.

Loyalty—Loyalty is absolutely essential to being a good follower and a great leader.

Communication—Both leaders and followers must communicate.

A leader is only as effective as his or her followers. If you consider yourself more of a follower than a leader, try and cultivate the traits of leadership while becoming a better follower.

Common Leadership Attributes

Thousands of books have been written about leadership and more speeches have been made about this than almost any other subject. It's true that great leaders possess certain characteristics that others just don't seem to have. Some experts think it's all about skills and talents while others think it takes charisma and trust to be a leader.

You may be great at coming up with ideas and plans for creating a successful business, but unless you have communication skills your great ideas may never come to fruition. Here are 10 attributes that are found in inspirational and successful leaders:

Organized —This attribute doesn't mean that you need a cubby hole for every paper, but you should be able to prepare yourself for presentations, meetings or whatever you're called to do in an organized fashion.

Motivator—Motivating a team to follow you means that you must be a positive person, willing to roll up your sleeves and do whatever you're asking others to do.

Respect—When you show respect for others, you're building respect and admiration for yourself. Treating those who serve you with respect is the mark of a true leader.

Flexibility—Unexpected situations arise. The merit of a leader depends on how they handle the unexpected and adapt to whatever adjustments need to be made.

Confidence—Exuding confidence even when you don't feel it inspires confidence in others. However, avoid becoming cocky.

Positive—While you can't keep a smile on your face 24/7, it is possible to look adversity in its face and still have a positive "can do" attitude. People look to positive-thinking people for guidance.

Communicate—Ask questions so that you can consider which options are available for a solution and then be ready to act on a decision.

Sense of Humor—Maintaining a light and humorous attitude about things help others feel good about themselves and helps to keep up morale. Laughing or making a joke about a broken copier is better than yelling at it.

Consistency—Rather than developing an up-and-down personality, good leaders are consistent in how they handle problems.

Initiator—A true leader is also an initiator who grabs the reins of a task or project and keeps it on track. He implements new projects and ideas and keeps the enthusiasm high.

When you recognize the exceptional attributes in leaders you admire, you can emulate them in yourself and become the leader who will inspire people and become successful in whatever you do.

Develop a "Win-Win" Mentality

Having a win-win mentality doesn't mean that you have to go around pleasing everyone. Working with others does require some give and take. Negotiation is a good way to work together for the greater good. When you negotiate, you're discussing a situation and what you're willing to do to make a sale happen.

Sometimes the negotiations go your way and sometimes not, but whatever the discussion, at least you'll have input. A win-win situation should be a cooperative effort rather than one of competition. Keep discussing until you find a way.

Develop the Courage to Lead

It takes courage to be a leader. Each decision you make in your personal and business life is a testament to your courage. Something as simple as refusing a rich dessert because you want to stay fit takes a certain amount of courage if you have gnawing cravings for sugar.

Other decisions you must make may be monumental and require the courage of a lion. A decision to quit a high-paying job to follow your life's dream is a major decision that takes courage and planning. Some decisions may seem unimportant in the moment, but later you may see that they were life changing.

Courage promotes confidence and self-esteem and builds a framework in which you can accomplish pretty much anything you set out to do. Think of the genius, Stephen Hawking, and how much he overcame to become one of the leading scientists and writers of our time.

Working through your greatest fears to have the courage to do something remarkable can lead you to success. Here are some steps you can take in your own life to help you build your courage to accomplish anything:

Create a positive environment—Surround yourself with people who are positive and who believe in you. You need those people who will bolster your self-confidence and increase your self-worth.

Maintain a positive attitude—Dealing with issues that challenge you can be turned into an opportunity for success. Try to think of each challenge in your life as an opportunity to use your skills and instincts to overcome and triumph.

Get out of your comfort zone—You'll never develop courage if you're in a rut. Each day, try something challenging and outside of what you normally do.

Don't let fear hold you back—Humans can become fearful of anything. Even situations that are supposed to be happy can become fearful if you overthink the situation. Get rid of those "what ifs" in your mind and replace them with positive thoughts.

Enjoy the struggle—Yes, you can enjoy the challenges if you know that they're building the courage that will spur you on to bigger and better things.

Each time you accomplish something or overcome a fear, your confidence will grow stronger. The courage of a true leader is accomplished by taking small steps rather than overcoming one big challenge, so take the steps to build your courage and be amazed at the results.

Be an Inspirational Leader

Whether you aspire to be an inspiration to a business, a congregation, or your kids, you should know that there are some common practices that inspirational leaders adhere to.

If you think that free coffee and donuts in the break room is going to inspire your employees to come to work, you need to rethink your courses of action. An inspirational leader removes barriers and then joins in the work to get the job done.

Enthusiasm—When you express passion for what you're doing, others become ignited. You may not be enthused about a course of action your company is taking, but you can have enthusiasm about getting everyone onboard to make it happen.

Tell Stories—When you tell personal stories about your company or how people are helped by your involvement in, others will be inspired.

Communicate a Vision—Lower-level employees may not become inspired about a plan that's going to make the executives lots of money but they will become inspired when you communicate a vision of what it will do for them.

Honesty—No matter what the challenge, an inspirational leader will face it with honesty. If you've made a mistake that's affecting your business or your family, you should be honest and forthright and have a plan to overcome any adversity.

Ask yourself what inspires you to new heights or to overcome seemingly insurmountable obstacles. When you find the answer, you can experience peak performance because you'll know what it takes to get you there. When you know what inspires others, you can be the leader who takes others to greater heights than they ever imagined. Listen to others, know what inspires them and you can become the inspirational leader you want to be.

13

SELL YOURSELF: USE A GREAT STORY

As you create your sales materials, you may be at a loss over what to write so that it doesn't look likeall your competitors. You should always be on the lookout for something special that will make people sit up and take notice.

Now, what would work better than a great story? I'm not talking about Aesop's Fables, but if you could weave in a story about your product or how you started the business, it could add a great human factor to the presentation.

It's natural to think that you don't have a story but you can dig one out. Was there some hurdle before your product made it to market? Where did the jolt of inspiration for your product or business come from? How has your product made a big difference to people, maybe even changed their lives for the better? You might even get a testimonial from a customer and use it in your sales presentation. These things do work, there's no question about that.

The major plus about testimonials is that they are told by someone else and strike a better chord with the readers. In any case, stories work, whether they are your own or your customers.

Creating the Undeniable Need

People don't purchase things on a whim anymore. Everyone has become quite money conscious during the ongoing economic downturn. People have money, they're just being more cautious how they spend it. The frivolous spending habits that we saw years ago have been toned down. People want you to show them why they should buy something from you.

Whatever your sales pitch is—the sales page, a television commercial, a magazine or a newspaper advertisement—the focus should be on what the product can do for them. You have to tell them the benefits they can enjoy and what their money will buy them. When people are convinced that they are spending their money on something useful, they won't mind opening their wallets.

People don't see things that you don't tell them. You might be selling a steam iron, but until you actually outline the advantages of getting a steam iron, people won't think of buying one. People won't buy it just because it exists. However, if you make a bulleted list of benefits and showcase those points, people will buy it. You can actually hear people saying things like, "See, Dolores, now I won't have to bend when I iron clothes at home."

That's a funny example but people talk themselves into buying things when the benefits of it are outlined. They almost convince themselves to make the purchase.

Stamping Your Authority

This is where your actual sales expertise comes into play. Making a list of the benefits is common but you have to make it so special that your customers can't resist. One of the best ways to do that is to focus on how you and your product are better than the competition.

You began this step when you wrote the story. But now you have to put that in your readers' faces. Make them see what's so special about you. Outline your special expertise in the area. Tell them why you are better than the others; maybe it's the creativeness of your product or an added feature that makes it unique or maybe it's your enhanced support system.

Be as transparent as you can be. Use forums and blogs to sell yourself. Allow customers to interact with you. They'll soon understand that you are for real and that you have answers to their apprehensions. They become more convinced about you as a person and will feel more comfortable buying from you.

Creating the Sense of Urgency

If you've seen any sales pitches lately, you have noticed a "Do It Now" urgency. A great ad for a great product for a great price will end with "This offer is only for three days. Do it Now!" The smiling blonde on Home TV will demonstrate a product that you absolutely want for your house and then say, "These prices are only until the next full moon" or something like that. Even the nerdy geek who puts his picture on the sales page creates a "Do It Now" scenario by stating that his prices have been dropped to $27 for only the next 24 hours. The truth is, his product never sold above $27.

When you tell people they're getting a bargain, they are always interested. We are all tickled when we bag a deal and it massages our ego when we have gotten a "bargain".

Even the big name malls and supermarkets publish ads for their hourly discounted sales. If you promote your offers well, you will get a good number of buyers. However, there are a few rules:

Your product needs to be good.

The bargain has to be attractive. If you only knock 50 cents off your price, it isn't going to mean anything.

The window of time should be short. If they have a few days to consider, they will not buy. At the same time, the time shouldn't be so short that they think your offer is a scam.

Make a Commitment

People who want to buy want to make sure that you will be there for them. They want to see your commitment. No one likes fly-by-night purchases in which they lose all contact with the seller. This might work if you're selling something for a dollar, but for most things that people buy, they want to see the seller remain involved even after the sale has been completed.

There is reason for that. They want to make sure that if anything goes wrong with the product, there is some remedy. Only the seller can ensure such a remedy. Take a look at a sales page on the Internet and you will find that there is almost always a money-back guarantee which sometimes extend to up to 90 days.

You must also provide a good money-back guarantee with a long enough period that people are convinced they can use the product and return it if they aren't satisfied.

Most likely they will never return your product. People are already very discerning when they buy and if you make everything quite clear, they will know exactly what to expect. Be honest and you will have few product returns.

What people want more than a money-back guarantee is a support system that continues after the product has been purchased. Most people aren't technically savvy and if your product requires the customer to use some kind of technical knowledge, you should be there to guide them. You have to promise your support even after the purchase is done.

Be honest and upfront about these promises and deliver them. This ensures long-term prospects for your business.

Keep the Interest Factor Alive

Not many people are going to buy things from you right away. In the offline world, it's much more likely to have people purchase when they walk into the store, but when it comes to expensive things the rate of conversion is low.

So, what must you do to clinch the deal in such cases? The most important thing you must do is to keep the interest factor alive. Build a list for people who don't buy immediately. These people might purchase, but they want that push before doing so. When you have them on the list, you can keep promoting to them through email and newsletters.

Make sure you send them quality material that will interest them. Research the kind of material that drives this particular niche. They might want to know more about DIY or receive weekly tips. Whatever it is they want to know, keep giving it to them at regular intervals. The idea is to keep them hooked. When one of your meaningful emails arrives in their inbox, dwindling interest might get a shot in the arm.

You might even consider inviting them to download an eBook or sign up for a free newsletter subscription. You might even enlist another marketer to give away things with you.

Quest to Become Perfect

No one can be a perfect salesperson because, despite your best efforts, there are always people who won't buy your product. There are many things that come into play and you need not take your failures personally. It's not always about your product or about you.

Improvement comes through practice. The more you try to sell, the more you learn. You learn what works and what doesn't. You learn what type of customer you can sell to and what type you can't. You learn who will keep buying from you and who will just be a drifter. You learn how to open your dialogue to make the maximum impact on a potential customer.

It's very important not to let failures bog you down. Keep on with your efforts and remember these points:

There's no guarantee that someone will buy from you, regardless of the efforts you put into making the sale. However, you can increase the chances of them buying by making your product more attractive for them.

Whatever it is, your product won't last. Keep improving it with new versions and updates.

Every failed sale teaches you something.

Learn how other sales people market their products. In fact, buy from them. See what convinces people to buy from them.

Keep improving. Keep evolving. You will be a better salesperson tomorrow than you are today just because you kept trying. Selling isn't difficult. You only need to know what ticks. Experience teaches you that wonderfully.

14

NETWORKING

When used wisely and appropriately, networking is one of your most cost-effective business building tools. But, don't approach it as a method to sell. Networking is the process of creating relationships where you can help each other achieve your goals.

Networking know-how is very important for your business success. There is a notion that I believe most of us subscribe to that says, all things being equal, people will do business with and refer business to those they know, like and trust. The key to this is obviously being able to develop relationships.

Think of networking as the cultivation of mutually beneficial, win-win relationships. In order to be win-win, there must be GIVE and take (notice the emphasis on give). Networking shouldn't be viewed simply as hanging out at events where you sell your business. Effective networking takes place when both parties actively share ideas, information, and resources.

Networking is one of the most cost-effective lead generation activities when used wisely, appropriately and professionally. Here's a 7-step plan to engage in business networking.

Check out several groups—You're looking to find the best chemistry and perceived value. Most groups will allow you to visit as a guest at least a couple of times. Ask around to find out why others have joined and what value they get out of belonging.Resist the urge to just go join the Chamber of Commerce simply because everyone tells you that's what you need to do. If that's not where your target group can be found, you'll be wasting a considerable amount of time and money.

Attend all the meetings you can—Don't go just once or twice expecting things to happen and then quit if they don't. Building mutually beneficial, win-win relationships will take some time.The contacts you make need to see your face and hear your message more than once. Continual contact over time will open up opportunities for you to go deeper and learn more about each others thoughts, ideas and capabilities in regards to your respective businesses. Trust generally happens only over time. Being regular and persistent will pay off.

Get involved and be visible—Do as much as you can to make yourself more visible within the organization. Volunteer to help with meetings, be on committees, or become a leader or board member.Being involved gives you more opportunities to establish connections and get to know your contacts even better. Secondly, the higher the visibility you have, the less you have to work to make new connections. Instead, as new people come into the group, they will likely seek you out because they view you as a leader within the organization.

Keep your contacts informed—Don't assume that running into someone once a month (or even once a week) will cause them to start doing business with you or sending it your way. You need to let them know what's going on in order to inform and educate them.Send them invitations to your events or open houses. Send them email or letters to share big news or success stories, especially anything of relevance to them or those within their networks of contacts. If you believe that you have valuable ideas, information and resources to share with others, then doesn't this just make sense?

GIVE referrals and share information—That's right, you need to be willing to GIVE before you get. That means you need to get to know other members and what makes a good prospect for them. What kinds of information might you have access to that could be useful to them?You may initially think you don't have much of value to share with others (besides your business and what you provide). The key, though, is to not make assumptions. Don't assume that something that you're aware of is familiar to someone you meet just because they are an expert in that field. Be willing to ask if they know about the resource and be ready to share if they don't.Want to get better at actually giving referrals? Here's a simple question to ask. "How am I going to know when I meet a really good prospect for you?" Just the fact that you are willing to explore giving will elevate your know, like and trust factor.

Focus on Quality, not Quantity—It's not the number of connections you make, but the quality. Are they mutually beneficial, win-win relationships? Quality connections will be identifiable because all involved parties will be actively sharing ideas, information, and resources. Yes, it is true that you need to spend some time and effort getting to know the other person and what's important to them. But, you also need to be clear and actively thinking about what information or resources you want and need.Staying in touch with and following up with a smaller number of quality relationships will generally be much more productive than trying to follow up with a larger number of superficial contacts.

Be persistent, but be patient—The goal of a networking group shouldn't necessarily be to come away with prospects every meeting, but to leave with great connections. Good networking usually takes time to develop and nurture relationships.

Don't approach networking as a scary proposition or a necessary evil. Take the pressure off yourself and focus on how you might be able to connect with someone you meet. Focus on them first and look for ways to be useful to them. As you become known as a connector, you'll eventually be ready to reap what you sow.

Networking on LinkedIn

LinkedIn.com is a business-focused social media network that claims more than 150 million users, most of whom have advanced education degrees and either work for a company or have their own business.

Perfect Your Profile

Before you even think of connecting and networking on LinkedIn, perfect your profile. The profiles on LinkedIn can be very extensive and serve as a powerful resume. Along with your typical resume, you also can add video, slideshows, links to websites and portfolios. You may also give and ask for recommendations and endorsements.

LinkedIn also features many groups where people connect, have discussions, answer questions and network. Search for groups that will either help you connect with customers or help you connect with others who can lead you to customers.

Be a Resource to Others

Nowthatyou'vegotafewconnectionsandarecommunicating in groups, start sharing important and relevant information. Start by being a resource to others. If you find a great article that would resonate with people in a particular group, share it and ask for commentary to start a discussion. If you write something, create a video, or design an infographic, share it and ask for comments.

Create networking goals that make sense for your business. For instance, you might make it a goal to meet at least one new local person local each month, or to connect with five new relevant people each week on LinkedIn, and make at least one introduction each month. If you carve out the time to use LinkedIn wisely, it can be a very powerful and productive business networking tool.

15

PERSONAL DEVELOPMENT

How you look matters. Reflect on your close friends and family members and who you think is ahead of the game of life. How does their appearance project success? A relevant aspect of portraying success is your image, which is a compilation of your personal appearance, how you behave, and your attitude. If you want to project success to others, follow the tips below.

Your Physical Body

Take a thorough look at your physique. If you were to see someone whose body looked like yours, would you consider them as successful?

Your skin/facial complexion—Is your skin clear or do you have acne or patches of dry, flaky skin?

Your teeth—Because your teeth are integral to your smile (not to mention good health), how do they look? Do you need dental care? Maybe you would benefit from using an over-the-counter whitening product at home.

Your hair—Maintain neat and clean hair. Regular, consistent haircuts and colorings (if you use them) contribute to looking your best.

Shape of your body—Looking at your own physique honestly and without judgment can be a real challenge. However, if you can do it with an honest, open heart and diplomacy, you'll be able to tackle the areas that trouble you.

Overall upkeep of your body—Taking time for the final touches contributes to your confidence and a successful look.

What changes should you make, if any? If your skin is clear, your teeth are healthy and white, and you're proud of your body and how well you maintain it, then you're on your way to looking successful.

Your Behavior

Evaluating your own behavior isn't easy. Take a closer look at how you act around your customers, family members, friends, and co-workers.

Your conduct is the key—Although the meaning of the words "lady" and "gentleman" has morphed over the years, think about how people might view you. If you had to sum up your behavior in one word, what would that be?

Do you verbally express yourself well?—Do you speak with articulation with proper speech and grammar? Your verbal expression "tells the tale" of how successful you are.

Do you display good listening skills?—A successful person is more focused on listening to what others have to say rather than doing all the talking. The ability to listen is important for those who strive to be successful.

Make it a point to take care of business—If you are efficient in your personal and professional life, you'll appear more successful.

Keep things around you neat and organized—When you can quickly retrieve what you're looking for and work in a well-maintained office, you get things done more quickly. Being neat and organized is often an important aspect of success.

When it comes to looking successful, your behavior matters. How you conduct yourself illustrates your true level of success.

Your Attitude

Finally, your approach to life, or your attitude, is an integral part of appearing (and being) successful.

Do you think positively?—A successful person is compelled to move forward in life. Thinking positively makes this possible.

Use tact and diplomacy—Make it a goal to use a business-like attitude when approaching others. You'll accomplish far more this way.

Show care and concern toward others—The attitude you portray toward others will contribute to your own success. Treating others as equals and being concerned about them can even draw others to you.

Your attitude is important to your success. Thinking positively, using tact and diplomacy and demonstrating care toward others are elements to possess when you're in front of a client. If you want to be successful, you must look the part. If you take care of your body, consider your own behavior, and maintain a positive attitude, you're likely to look and be successful as well.

What to Look For in a Mentor

Before deciding to seek out a mentor, you must first determine what you hope to gain from the relationship. That means you need to spend time thinking about both your short and long term goals. Once you're fully clear on where you want to be, the selection process becomes that much easier.

When people think about mentors, they often visualize a classic business setting, where everything is formal and methodical, but mentoring relationships aren't limited to business. The truth is, you may desire a mentor for any number of reasons.

Life Guidance—These life mentors are often referred to as "life coaches."

Spiritual Advisors—You can look to a priest, pastor, or friend to mentor you spiritually.

Everyday Mentors—Sometimes we have unofficial mentors who are simply people we admire in our community or peer group.

Choosing a Mentor

I've learned from many sales trainers; there wasn't just one person who taught me everything. The knowledge came from some of the best sales people and trainers and pastors I've listened to in church. Whether they're in real estate or marketing or whatever, I can learn from a person who lives with passion, who is focused and committed, with discipline and good follow-through and who loves what he does. If he loves people and loves to make a difference; I consider that person a mentor. There's so many to name whom I've admired that it wouldn't be fair to give the "LeBron title" to any one.

When looking for a mentor, seek someone who possesses the qualities, skills, and experiences you hope to have yourself someday. A mentor should be someone who fits your idea of success, has a positive attitude, and openly shares their knowledge with you.

You might want a mentor who's at the pinnacle of success within your field so you can learn from the best. Or, you might want to select someone who's only slightly higher ranking than you so you can learn what you need to move to the next level.

Choosing the high ranking executive helps you with long term goals, while selecting the peer mentor makes it easier to focus on a specific expertise so you can achieve your shorter term goals.

An ideal situation may involve both types of mentors. This way you get a well-rounded experience that allows you to benefit both in the short and long term. Either way, you should find someone who isn't afraid to challenge you to reach your true potential.

Establishing a Beneficial Relationship

When you've selected your mentor candidate, draw up a plan detailing what you hope to give and receive from the relationship. This will help the potential mentor decide if they can provide you with the experience and knowledge you desire. It's only fair to both of you to be as upfront as possible about your expectations. If you aren't clear on what you hope to gain, the relationship has little chance for success.

Successful Mentorship Begins with You

Once the relationship has been established, actively communicate your needs to the mentor in order to take the sessions in the direction you'd like to go. You should be in the driver's seat, even though you're the junior party in the relationship. Without providing your mentor with guidance, the mentorship may not be fruitful for you. After all, if you don't let your mentor know what you need, he can't possibly give you what you hope to gain.

It's important throughout the relationship for the mentor to be supportive. A good mentor will be patient with you and will create an open and welcome environment that allows for earnest questions and concerns while making you feeling safe. A successful mentorship will enable you to feel more confident, skilled, and knowledgeable. The reward for the mentor will be seeing the results of the positive impact they were able to make on someone else's life.

Follow these tips to find great mentors in any area you'd like to strengthen and enjoy a relationship that brings fruits to your labor and greater life fulfillment to both of you.

16

FUNDAMENTAL SALESMANSHIP

Many salesmen believe that, since they are selling a genuine quality product, people will naturally buy it. It sounds good, but it simply isn't true. You have to sell yourself as well as the product. People buy the salesman not the product. Most customers will remember a good salesman for years. I still run into customers from years ago who still remember me.

Psychology is the biggest part of selling. Knowing how the mind works and reacts to certain things is a great asset for any salesman. There are little things you can do that can have a powerful impact on the customer. For example, did you know that not having your own pen could jeopardize the closing of a deal?

Nearly 90% of my sales calls begin with the customer telling me no. We can hear a thousand no's, but all we need is one yes. People's natural reaction to anything is to say no. Yes is a word that suggests commitment, and we all know people naturally have a fear of commitment.

People generally don't like to be sold. I could be selling a cure for asthma to someone in dire need, but if he feels as if I'm putting on a sales pitch, he won't buy it. Simply put, it's about getting straight to the point. Many salesmen believe you need to make small talk when selling to a customer. I also had this belief when I started selling. Halfway through my sales pitch I'd know their whole family by name, their occupations, and the last time they took a family vacation. I was practically part of the family. The problem was when it was time to buy I still wasn't getting the sale. Becoming friends with the customer doesn't hurt the sale; it just doesn't help it as much as many believe.

The truth is the only person who can make you a better salesman is YOU. You don'thave to be some flamboyant smooth-walking, slick-talking person in order to beeffective. Being yourself with a positive attitude is good enough.

If you went to see your doctor, and he prescribed a particular over-the-counter drug or a particular type of food, chances are you would listen to his advice. Why is it that when a doctor recommends a product, people buy it without any hesitation?

The main reason is people respect and trust their doctors and see them as experts. The relationship between a doctor and patient is built on trust and developed over time. Therefore a doctor doesn't need to sell anything; he simply has to recommend something and people will do it.

Unfortunately, for sales people, it isn't that easy. You need to discover a few ways to command the respect of your customers so that they'll see you as an authority on the products you sell. Customers want two basic things.

Quality service—In other words, they expect your product or service to work, to do what you say it'll do.

Friendly, caring attention—They want to be acknowledged, to feel that someone is interested in them as an individual and that they're cared about.

First impressions are vital, therefore, it makes good sense to consider what you lookand sound like. In a face-to-face situation it's important to make eye contact and smile. On the telephone, your initial greeting is important.

Always be warm and friendly because this is what most people want and it makes your life easier too.

A person's name is one of the warmest sounds they hear. It says that you have recognized them as an individual. Therefore, use names appropriately.

Most people aren't very good listeners. We'd all rather be talking but you have to work hard at listening if you want to let the other person know that you care.

If a customer says something, the intention was for you to hear it. If you hear it, it's a good idea to respond to it.

At the end of an interaction it's a good idea to make a positive statement on a business level and a personal level.

Make no mistake about it, providing friendly caring service creates that little bit extra and generates word of mouth for your business.

Gaining trust

Work at getting your customer to trust you. Begin by getting to know your customer and look for things that you might have in common. Let them know that building a relationship with them is more important to you than the products you sell.

Listen carefully to them and explain everything in plain English so that they can understand. Don't be pushy, let them go at their own pace, but keep the conversation going. The more time you spend with your customer, the better. When they get to know you better, they begin to trust you.

Product knowledge

Know your products by studying them inside out. Your customer is going to want to know what your product can do for them, how it will make their lives easier, or how it can save them money. They aren't concerned about your weekly or monthly goals.

If a customer wants to know something about your product, be prepared to answer. Would you buy a product from someone who didn't know anything about their product? I wouldn't.

Be accessible

Always be available to your customer; give them your cell number as well as your office number. By giving them your cell number you have just taken your first step to personalizing your business relationship. Make your customers understand that you are available to answer any questions or to discuss any concerns they may have.

Remember, building relationships is about trust. If your customers trust you, then they will do business with you. If your customers like you and trust you, they will most likely refer family and friends to you.

What is Selling?

Eighty percent of all communication is devoted to selling something to someone. Many people lack general knowledge of the how-to techniques and principles of sales but, with the right kind of training, all these techniques are learnable. Once learned, implemented and mastered, professional selling skills will enhance your business.

Selling is the ability to get a decision in your favor.

Selling is the ability to get someone else to do something you want them to do because you've convinced them they want to do it.

Selling is the ability to communicate your product's technical features and benefits so your prospect can make an intelligent decision to buy.

Professionalism versus High Pressure

Professionals have specific skills and expertise to call upon to serve their clients. They think in terms of their prospects' interests first, last and always. High-pressure salespeople, on the other hand, think in terms of their own interests first, last and always. High-pressure techniques can include:

- Speaking down to a prospect

- Overly persistent

- Rudeness

- Impatience

Enthusiasm

Enthusiasm is an emotion that can be electrifying and inspiring. It is an essential characteristic of a successful sales person and should be present in every appointment, presentation and training session. Sales enthusiasm is based on two factors:

- Sufficient knowledge of your product or service.

- Belief in the goodness your product or service provides for your prospects.

Empathy

Empathy is the ability to put yourself in the other person's shoes. The most important obligation any professional salesperson has is to develop the ability to be empathetic with the prospect. This skill requires you to become an exceptional listener. Don't confuse empathy with sympathy, which is putting yourself in the prospect's shoes and agreeing with them or feeling sorry for them.

Closing Techniques

Alternate proposal—Offering a prospect a choice.

"Would meeting Wednesday or Saturday be better?"

"Which do you prefer, an insurance policy with more risk but higher returns or one with low risk and steady returns?"

"We need to schedule your medical exam next week. Which day works best?"

Triplicate of Choice—Give your prospect multiple choices.

"Many of the people I work with save $20 per day through this insurance program. There are some exceptional people who can afford to save $40-$50 per day. Which category do you fit into?"

Benjamin Franklin Close—Drawing a line in the middle of a piece of paper and writing down the advantages and disadvantages.

"Whenever Ben Franklin had to make a decision he would draw a line in the middle of a blank sheet of paper and write down the reasons for and the reasons against a decision. He'd then add up both sides and go with the one with the most answers. Let's try that together."

You give all the reasons why they should join the company or own the product you are offering. Then let the prospect come up with all the disadvantages (don't help them with this).

The sharp angle close—It's great when a prospect asks how soon you can complete a medical exam or approve them into the system. Remain silent after you ask the prospect to move forward with the application.

Prospect: "If I decide to buy this insurance policy, I would need to have the medical exam done by January 15. Can you handle that?"

You: "If I could guarantee your medical to be done by January 15, is there any other reason not to move forward with the application today?"

Reduce the Pain—Taking an amount of money and dividing down to a very small daily amount.

Prospect: "Four-hundred a month seems like a lot of money."

You: "Well let's break that down. Four hundred per month divided by four equals one hundred per week. One hundred per week divided by seven days equals seventeen dollars a day. Is saving seventeen dollars a day too much? How about if I reduce it to fifteen dollars a day?"

Ask for the Sale

Many sales people will get to that critical point where all they need to do is ask for the sale...but then they freeze. How important is that ability to pull the trigger and ask for the sale even if you have a pretty good inkling the answer is going to be No?

Well, for me, I never assume that I can't serve that person. Whenever I'm in a sales position my question is not how do I close, it's how do I serve. If I look at my position as a servant leader, I never really worry about closing as much as I care about serving. The reason why guys aren't successful is because they're trying too hard to close someone. I think it's been a magic sales word for many years, "I closed a sale" or "Did you close?" or "Did you close the deal?" These are things that most sales people assume is the ultimate goal. But in the new world that we're in, I think we all know that sales means influence. Sales means leadership.

For me, a sale is based on influence and a chance at serving. Am I serving this family? This is what you asked me to do, this is what I believe will serve you the most, let's go ahead and get this started. Now, there is a point at which I will lead a client. I believe that most people have a harder time saying No than saying Yes. If you ever have someone go to your house and try to sell you a Kirby vacuum or a set of knives and they actually get a chance to sit in front of you, you'll notice there's a little part of you that feels bad about saying No.

It's very difficult to say No to someone who's working really hard to help you. If you do a great job of serving this individual, this family, this client, it'd be very difficult for them to say No. It's very easy to say No when the sales person hasn't done much work. But when you've overserved, closing becomes simpler.

Now, are there techniques and strategies to closing? Sure, there's influential ways to get things done. How to say things, how you talk, how you ask. Ultimately you have to ask, but the best of the best come across as if they're not asking, but they get it anyway. They just assume it. I always assume that, after all I've done, you're going to move forward. I don't say, "Are you going to buy?" After all the information I share with you, I believe this is the best. I agree, let's move forward.

15 Ways to Increase Customer Satisfaction

Customer satisfaction is one of the most important segments of any business. Learning how to deal with your customers the right way will increase your customer satisfaction, build a community that trusts you, and lead to a bigger bottom line. Training your team members to increase customer satisfaction is key in building good relationships. Here are 15 key ways to increase customer satisfaction:

1. Listen to what they have to say. Some clients just need to rant, even if they are in the wrong. Don't take it personally and always respond in a professional manner.

2. Don't refer the person to someone else. No one likes to get the runaround and be shoved off onto someone else. Get the answers the client needs ASAP.

3. Keep your promises. Only agree to what you can actually deliver. Telling the client you can deliver more than you can stresses you and you lose the customer's trust.

4. Under-promise and over-deliver whenever possible.

5. Be courteous. Thank your customer for their business. Let them speak without interrupting.

6. Develop personal relationships with your clients. Treat each one as if he's your most important client.

7. Anticipate their needs. Go the extra step and be ahead of them.

8. Apologize if you are wrong or make a mistake. Everyone makes them.

9. Respond quickly to communications. One working day turnaround time should be a top priority for all customer inquiries.

10. Be honest. If a requested deadline can't be met, let your client know before you take their order.

11. Keep in touch with the customer. Follow up with a postcard, an email or a simple thank you phone call.

12. Ask for feedback from your customers. They will give you information to help you improve your customer service and your business reputation.

13. Listen to what your unsatisfied customers have to say. Act on their advice if it is the right thing to do.

14. Smile. Be happy and courteous. Never answer the phone or email when you're angry. Before you pick up the phone, put a smile on your face and in your voice.

15. Throw away your scripts. People want to hear from real people who treat them like individuals. Each situation is different so you shouldn't have a pre-written script.

17

WORKING IN THE SALES BUSINESS IS...

...whatever you want it to be. You know, one of the things that I utilize sales for is the freedom of expression. I believe that a salesperson gets a chance to express himself while others don't often do. The sales business has no ceilings over how great you can become. You have no limits for how much money you can make or how much you can learn. There is no glass ceiling in sales. You create your own ceiling based on your own work ethic.

A sales career is also a personal development business where you're always trying to grow. It can also make a difference in others as you teach and develop the next generation of sales people to have the same habits and character and focus that you did.

I think being in sales is one of the greatest feelings because it makes such a difference in the world. There isn't anything that people buy without someone to sell it, whether it's a car, or a television, or a house, or a vacation package. Everything has had someone of influence sell it to you.

What this country needs is more influential sales people who really care about others and have good intentions, not just to make money but for the ultimate good of humanity. I believe just having a good heart and helping people achieve their goals and dreams is one of the greatest gifts of a sales career.

Putting it all Together

You have been given the information necessary to become an Intellectual Salesman and now it's time to put it all together to make it work for you. In my opinion, the following items are not optional. They are REQUIRED for you to succeed in becoming ELITE. This is not easy; in order to reach elite status, you must understand that it will require CHANGE and it might HURT! You've heard the phrase, "No Pain, No Gain?" It may not hurt physically but it could hurt mentally!

CLARITY - Are you clear on your mission? Are you crystal clear on what it is that you want? You cannot go to step 2 without knowing what you want! "I want to be self-employed!" "I will lose 20 pounds of body fat!" "I want to make $10,000 this week, I want to begin my classes!" Without CLARITY you have nothing!

STRATEGY - Now that you know what you clearly want, what is your Plan? What is your strategy? How are you going to do it? An Intellectual Salesman will know his STRATEGY! For example, if you decide to lose 20 pounds of body fat, how many times will you work out per week? What will your diet be? How many hours will you invest in your fitness? What supplements will you need? What exercises will you perform and which days will you perform them? What intensity? When will you do cardio? When will you do weights? What time of the day? Morning, evenings, weekends? Strategy is the essence of the Intellectual Salesman. What is your plan? How will you execute? How will you monitor progress? Who will monitor your progress? How will you know if you're growing?

INTEGRATION – Stop talking and finish what you started! The Intellectual Salesman is all about completion, integration and commitment. Are you ready to complete what you started? Are you ready to get passionate about what you do? Integration is necessary to allow success into your current schedule. You must allow your strategy to work by integrating it into your life. You will hear a lot of people talk about what they PLAN to do, but they rarely finish. Why? It's not because they did not have intentions, goals and dreams. It's that they lacked INTEGRATION. They forgot to integrate their strategy into their life. Without INTEGRATION, how do you expect to finish anything?

8 Intellectual Salesman Tips

Do you have detailed goals? If not, why not? must have goals!

Must have a detailed (DOCUMENTED) schedule from morning to evening.

- When do you get up?
- When do you prospect? How long? How many calls do you make?
- When do you exercise?
- When do you see clients?
- What are your hours of operation?

Must have follow through and monitor Progress

Must adjust your plan if your results are not progressing.

Do the majors first.

Prospecting

Contacting

Presentation

Focus on your strengths – If you're great at talking to people, go out and find new ways to meet new people.

Personal Growth and Development – Make every day matter by adding personal development. Listen to audio books, read books, attend seminars, events, trainings or anything that will help you grow. Personal Development is necessary to take your sales career to the next level. You must find a mentor to help guide you. You must become a mentor to help others achieve their dreams! You can only do that if you are growing.

You must focus on the major responsibilities of the elite:

- New prospects in your influnace daily
- Exsisting clients service
- Closing the Sale
- Getting Referrals

Focus on SERVING... It's not about CLOSING. It's about helping families reach their goals through you! Have a mindset of service. It's not about how much you sell, it's about how many you SERVE! Transform your business from Selling to SERVING!

Be GRATEFUL and HUMBLE – Grateful for your families, blessings, talents and gifts. Be humble that you are able to serve others as a career. Humble that you are able to provide for your family. Humble to be fortunate enough to help others do the same!

Get Excited! Life is about getting excited! You must enjoy the process of growing and learning. You must get passionate and excited! I have never seen anyone with passion not get excited about something. Be excited to wake up in the morning and start a new day with new experiences. Get excited about your future. Life is too short to feel down with daily issues, problems and challenges. I feel that this Bible verses sums it up. I wish you all success and blessing. God bless.

"For our present troubles are small and won't last very long. Yet they produce for us a glory that vastly outweighs them and will last forever. So we don't look at the troubles we can see now; rather, we fix our gaze on things that cannot be seen. For the things we see now will soon be gone, but the things we cannot see will last forever."- 2 Corinthians 4: 17-18

www.ingramcontent.com/pod-product-compliance
Lightning Source LLC
Chambersburg PA
CBHW062035200326
41519CB00017B/5045